DK

Earth's Incredible Habitats

Forest

Written by
Derek Harvey

Illustrated by
Federico Epis

Written by Derek Harvey
Illustrated by Federico Epis

Senior editor Kritika Gupta
Senior art editor Roohi Rais
US Senior editor Jennette ElNaggar
Editor Soumya Rampal
Art editors Mitravinda V K, Debjyoti Mukherjee, Mohd Zishan
Jacket designers Rashika Kachroo, Bettina Myklebust Støvne
Jacket coordinator Elin Woosnam
Senior picture researcher Sakshi Saluja
Picture researcher Ridhima Sikka
Preproduction image editor Nityanand Kumar
Preproduction designer Bimlesh Tiwary
Managing editor Roohi Sehgal
Managing art editors Diane Peyton Jones, Ivy Sengupta
Production editor Vishal Bhatia
Senior production controller Ena Matagic
Creative head Malavika Talukder
Publisher James Mitchem
Art director Mabel Chan

Consultant Dr. Michael Leach

First American Edition, 2026
Published in the United States by DK Publishing,
a division of Penguin Random House LLC
1745 Broadway, 20th Floor, New York, NY 10019

26 27 28 29 30 10 9 8 7 6 5 4 3 2 1
001–343438–Feb/2026

Published in Great Britain by Dorling Kindersley Limited

ISBN 978-0-5939-7196-3

DK books are available at special discounts when purchased in bulk for sales promotions, premiums, fund-raising, or educational use. For details, contact:
DK Publishing Special Markets,
1745 Broadway, 20th Floor, New York, NY 10019
SpecialSales@dk.com

Printed and bound in China

www.dk.com

This book was made with Forest Stewardship Council™ certified paper—one small step in DK's commitment to a sustainable future.
Learn more at www.dk.com/uk/information/sustainability

Contents

TEMPERATE FORESTS

TROPICAL FORESTS

North America

As the days shorten and summer turns to fall, forests along the eastern Atlantic coast of North America blaze with red and yellow. This is a time when maples and other deciduous trees prepare to shed their leaves for winter. In contrast, forests of the subarctic north and Pacific west are dominated by evergreen trees—with vast stretches of pines and firs and foggy valleys with giant redwoods.

South America

The Amazon basin is home to the largest rainforest in the world, fed by thousands of streams that pour water into the mighty Amazon River system. Other tropical forests in South America stretch north to the Caribbean, west through the Andes, and east along the Atlantic coast. This continent has an unrivaled variety of wildlife—from plants sprouting on tree limbs to hummingbirds flitting between vivid flowers and tarantulas creeping across the forest floor.

Europe

Scandinavia's conifers are part of a sprawling belt of forests that encircles the snowy Arctic. Further south, these evergreens give way to the ancient deciduous oak and beech woods in the British Isles and continental Europe. Though many of these southern woodlands have been cleared for towns, cities, and farmland, some forests still survive—where badgers, boars, and bears roam free.

Africa

The richest forests of Africa are in its equatorial heart, between the dry Sahara to the north and grassy savannas to the south. These rainforests are home to our closest primate relatives—gorillas, chimpanzees, and monkeys. To the east is the island of Madagascar, where our more distant cousins—lemurs—live in both wet rainforests and dry scrub.

Asia

The forests of Asia reveal a landscape of striking contrasts. Along some of its coasts, the arching roots of mangrove trees plunge into the sea. Inland, rainforests drip with year-round moisture and orangutans climb around the high treetops. Monsoon forests, home to prowling tigers, stretch across regions with long dry seasons. High in the Himalayas and northward in China, the cooler forests are home to rhododendrons, bamboos, and pandas.

Oceania

In the treetops of tropical New Guinea, a Raggiana bird-of-paradise spreads its dazzling plumage to attract a female. Rich in birdlife, these forests lie within Oceania, a region that includes Australia and the Pacific Islands. It extends southward through the eucalyptus woodlands of the outback to the cool rainforests of Tasmania and New Zealand.

What is a forest?

Forests are places where trees loom large—stretching skyward and shaping the world beneath them. When trees grow close together, their leaves and branches intermingle to form a leafy canopy that shades the life below. No other land habitat reaches so high from the ground or supports such diversity of plants and animals. From the forest floor to the treetops, every layer is full of life.

Trees and shrubs

Plants with woody stems and branches include trees and shrubs. Trees have a single upright trunk with branches at the top, while shrubs have many stems and spread out near the ground. In forests, treetops create a leafy roof, but woodlands have more open spaces. Shrubs grow more freely in woodlands. In areas where they are dominant, the habitat is called shrubland.

Dense forest

Open woodland

Shrubland

How trees work

Trees, like all other plants, rely on sunlight to fuel their lives. Their green leaves absorb the sun's energy and carbon dioxide gas from the air. This is combined with water and minerals from the soil to make food—a process called photosynthesis.

Forest communities

A habitat's community is made up of all its interacting species. Forests have especially complex communities because they shelter a wide variety of species. These include plant-eating animals and predators, as well as decomposers that feed on dead wood and fallen leaves.

Woody trunks

Trees use part of the food made through photosynthesis to make wood. New wood begins to form in the center of a stem or branch. Over time, the central tubes that transport food and water harden into supporting "heartwood."

Forest height

The tallest trees in the world grow in forest canopies, reaching heights of more than 328 ft (100 m). Most canopies, however, are 66–98 ft (20–30 m) high. These giants rise above their neighbors to reach more sunlight, but growing tall requires stronger supporting trunks, which increases their risk of toppling.

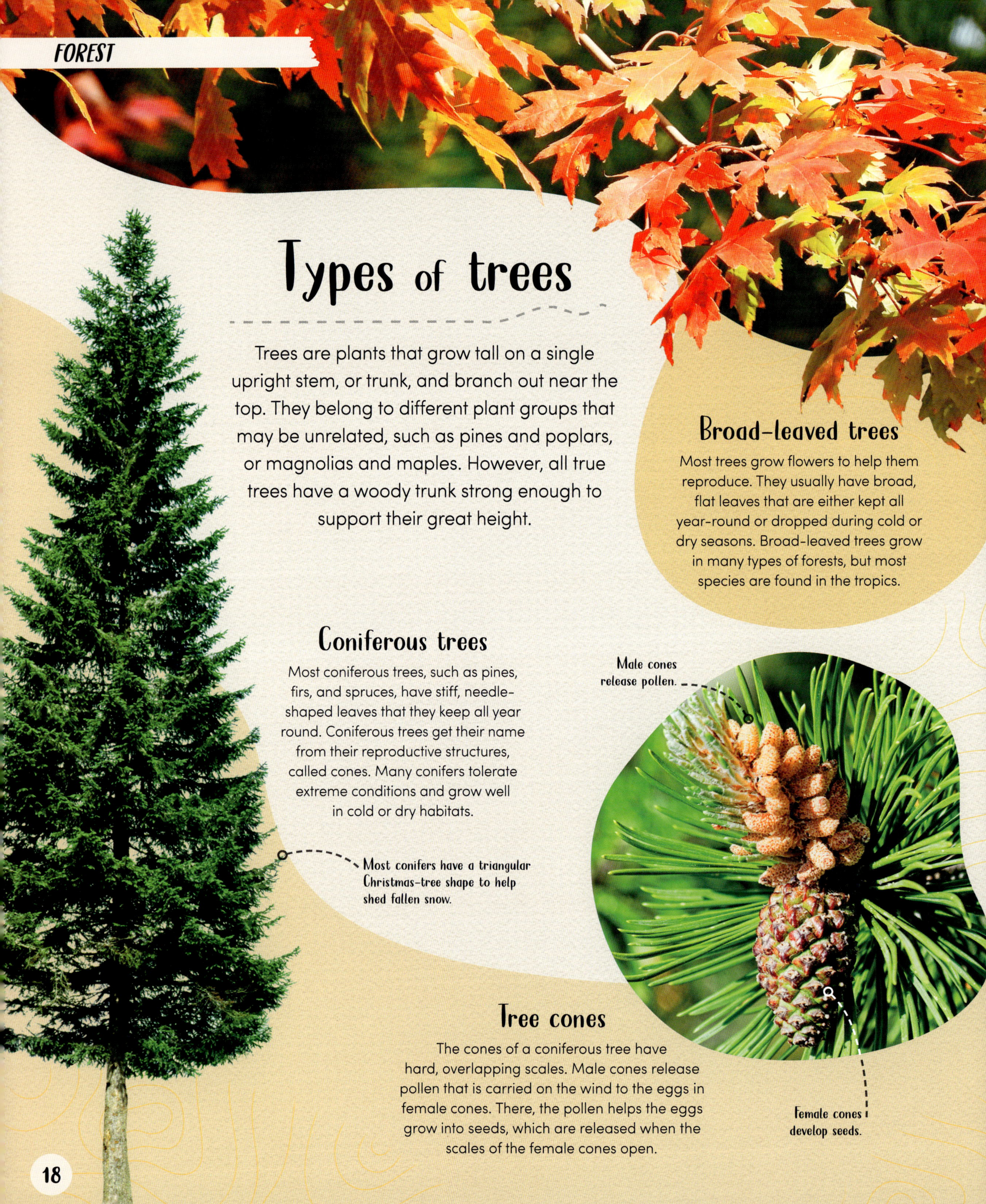

Types of trees

Trees are plants that grow tall on a single upright stem, or trunk, and branch out near the top. They belong to different plant groups that may be unrelated, such as pines and poplars, or magnolias and maples. However, all true trees have a woody trunk strong enough to support their great height.

Broad-leaved trees

Most trees grow flowers to help them reproduce. They usually have broad, flat leaves that are either kept all year-round or dropped during cold or dry seasons. Broad-leaved trees grow in many types of forests, but most species are found in the tropics.

Coniferous trees

Most coniferous trees, such as pines, firs, and spruces, have stiff, needle-shaped leaves that they keep all year round. Coniferous trees get their name from their reproductive structures, called cones. Many conifers tolerate extreme conditions and grow well in cold or dry habitats.

Tree cones

The cones of a coniferous tree have hard, overlapping scales. Male cones release pollen that is carried on the wind to the eggs in female cones. There, the pollen helps the eggs grow into seeds, which are released when the scales of the female cones open.

Surviving extremes

Trees can live for hundreds or thousands of years, and some survive in the harshest of environments. Desert trees draw water from deep underground using long roots and store it in thick trunks. Their small, leathery leaves reduce water loss from evaporation—the process in which water escapes into the air as it warms up.

Tree flowers

Some broad-leaved trees such as magnolia produce showy flowers to attract animals that help spread pollen. Others like oaks release pollen into the wind from smaller blooms. All develop seeds inside fruit, which may be hard, like an oak's acorn, or soft and fleshy, like an apple.

False trees

Some plants can grow tall without a woody trunk. Instead, they pack their thick stems with softer tissue. Banana plants, for instance, have a stem made from overlapping fleshy, leafy stalks.

Forests of the world

Forests grow wherever trees can survive, but different trees need different levels of warmth and moisture. This is why forests look so varied around the world. Some grow in the steaming tropics, others in icy lands with long, harsh winters. Some stay green year-round, while others endure months of harsh drought.

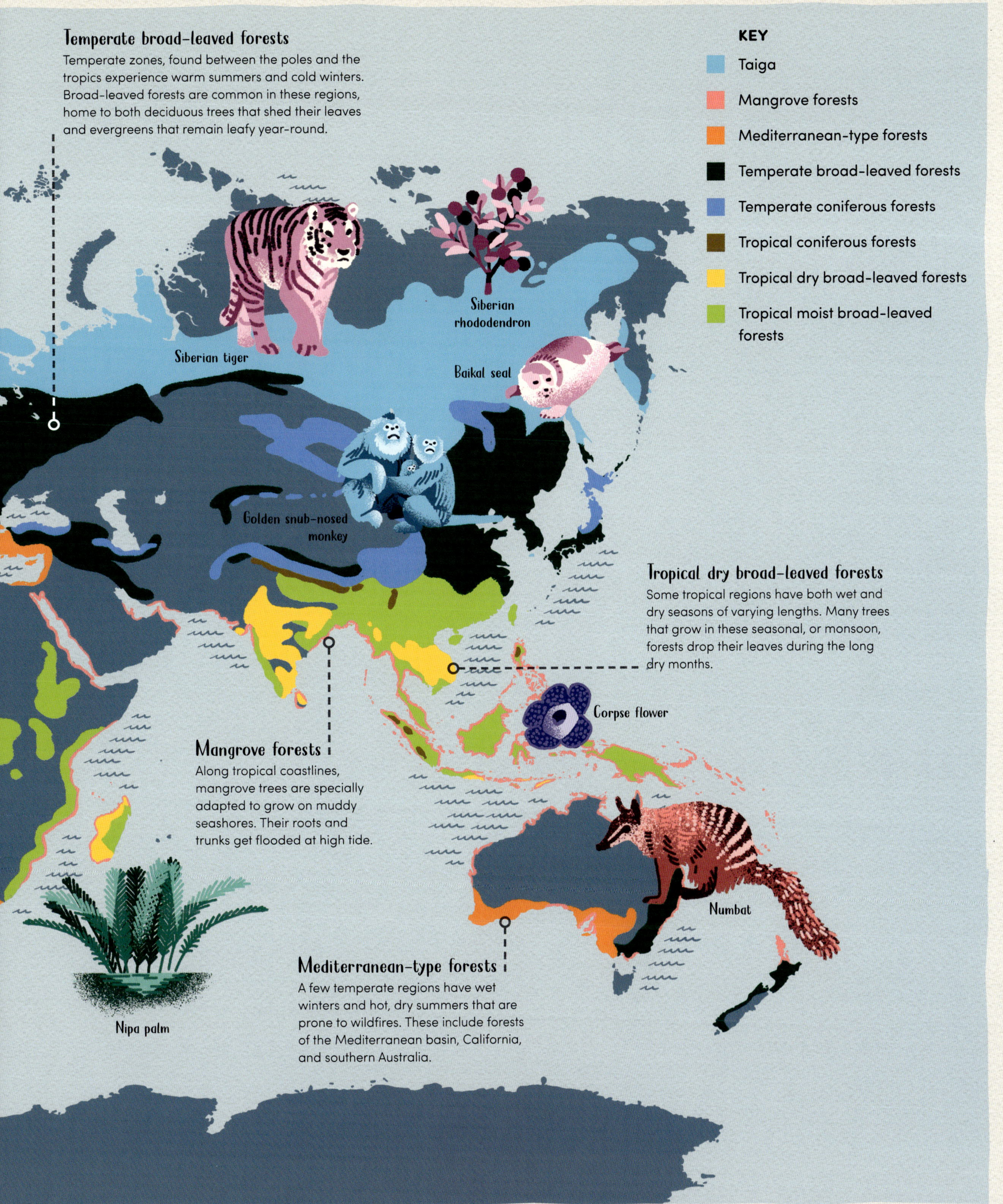
Temperate broad-leaved forests
Temperate zones, found between the poles and the tropics experience warm summers and cold winters. Broad-leaved forests are common in these regions, home to both deciduous trees that shed their leaves and evergreens that remain leafy year-round.
KEY
Taiga
Mangrove forests
Mediterranean-type forests
Temperate broad-leaved forests
Temperate coniferous forests
Tropical coniferous forests
Tropical dry broad-leaved forests
Tropical moist broad-leaved forests
Siberian rhododendron
Siberian tiger
Baikal seal
Golden snub-nosed monkey
Tropical dry broad-leaved forests
Some tropical regions have both wet and dry seasons of varying lengths. Many trees that grow in these seasonal, or monsoon, forests drop their leaves during the long dry months.
Corpse flower
Mangrove forests
Along tropical coastlines, mangrove trees are specially adapted to grow on muddy seashores. Their roots and trunks get flooded at high tide.
Numbat
Mediterranean-type forests
A few temperate regions have wet winters and hot, dry summers that are prone to wildfires. These include forests of the Mediterranean basin, California, and southern Australia.
Nipa palm

Forests and seasons

In seasonal parts of the world, many forests change as summer turns to winter or the rainy season gives way to drought. Evergreen trees keep their leaves year round, but deciduous trees need warmth and moisture to stay leafy. In cold or dry conditions, they shed their leaves, leaving once-green forests bare.

Summer and winter forests

In temperate forests, the changing seasons reshape the landscape. Oaks and beeches dominate these forests, filling the canopy with green in summer. As winter sets in, the trees shed their leaves, revealing bare trunks rising from a blanket of white snow.

Tropical monsoon

In summer, land heats up faster than the sea, causing warm air to rise and draw in moisture from the ocean. Over tropical regions, this forms thick clouds that drench the land with rain. Winters keep the land drier, with moisture out at sea. This seasonal rainfall is known as monsoon.

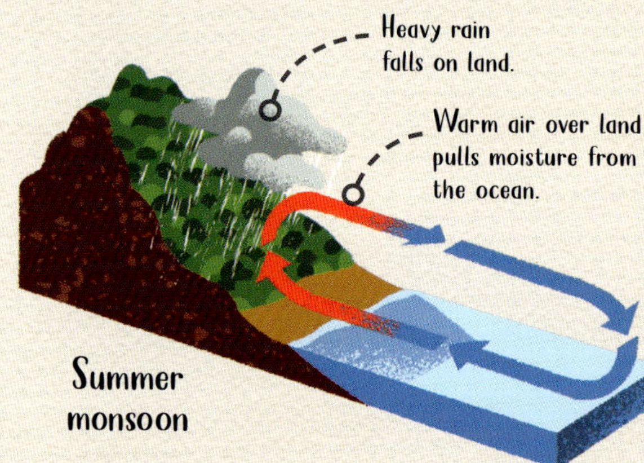

Monsoon forests

Some tropical areas have a monsoon climate, where a rainy season is followed by a drought. During the dry months, tropical deciduous trees typically lose most of their leaves. When the rains return, these forests burst back into green.

Mediterranean climate forests

A special type of climate occurs in the Mediterranean basin, California, Chile, South Africa, and southern Australia. Summers here are especially hot and dry. So many plants need to survive frequent wildfires, which are fanned by strong seasonal winds.

Rainforests and cloud forests

The heaviest rainfall occurs over rainforests, keeping the ground constantly wet. Some mountain forests catch moisture from clouds that often hang low over the trees. In these "cloud forests," plants can absorb as much water through their leaves as from the ground.

Nonseasonal forests

At the equator, seasonal changes are minimal, and conditions stay hot and rainy all year round. Animals remain active, and plants keep growing. So some birds can nest at any time of year, and some trees always bear fruit.

Okapis in the Congo rainforest can mate throughout the year.

Water and nutrient cycles

Plants absorb rainwater through their roots and pull it up through their stems. Some moisture evaporates from their leaves, helping form new rain clouds. Fallen leaves and other dead matter slowly break down, or decompose, releasing minerals back into the soil that living plants absorb.

Water cycle

Nutrient cycle

A few emergent trees grow higher than the canopy.

Most of the tallest trees form a closed canopy.

Shorter trees form an understory layer.

Nonwoody plants grow closer to the ground.

How forests work

Forests are complex habitats, with many different kinds of plants and animals living together. All these species are interconnected. Plants provide food and shelter for animals, while animals eat plants or each other. Living things also rely on the nonliving parts of the habitat—breathable air, underground soil, and moisture that falls as rain.

Forest layers

Plants need light to survive and grow, but not all can reach the height of the tallest trees. Some grow in the shade near the forest floor, while others stretch upward beneath the canopy. This variety gives the forest a layered structure.

Mycorrhizas

Fungi help decompose fallen leaves, but many also work with the roots of living trees. These fungus–root partnerships are called mycorrhizas. The fungus passes minerals to the tree's roots through fine threads. In return, the tree shares some of its sugar made through photosynthesis.

Leaf litter

All trees drop leaves. Deciduous trees shed them all at once in winter or the dry season. Evergreen trees lose leaves continuously as they age. Fallen leaves form a layer of litter on the forest floor and provide recycled nutrients for plants, fungi, and other tiny creatures that live in the soil.

Forest regeneration

Although trees can live for a very long time, none lasts forever. Eventually, a tree falls over, perhaps because it dies of old age or is blown down by the wind. This creates a light gap in the canopy, which is filled by younger trees growing underneath.

Threats

Forests are vital habitats for plants and animals. They help regulate the planet's climate and its nutrient and water cycles. Today, forests face many human-caused threats, including deforestation, pollution, and global warming. Fortunately, conservation efforts are helping to reverse some of this damage—by planting trees and protecting the life that depends on them.

Deforestation

Forests are cleared as trees are cut down for their wood, which is used in construction or as fuel. This process, called deforestation, also happens when people clear natural habitat to make room for farms, towns, and cities.

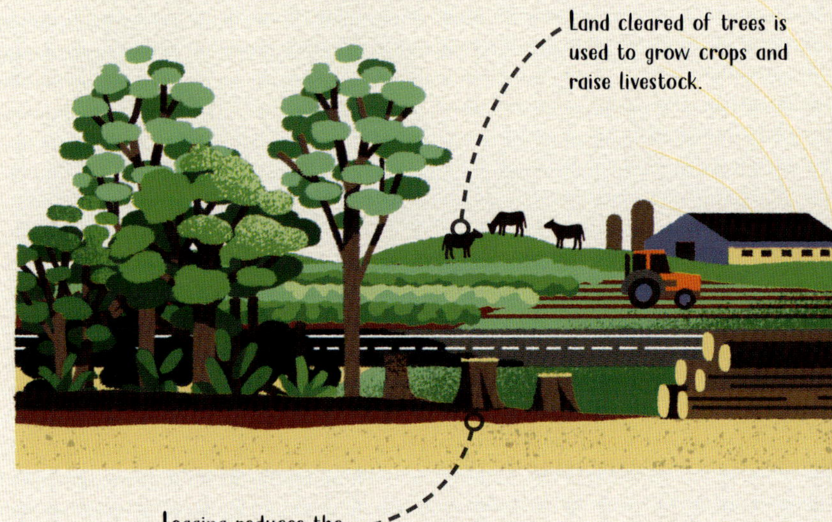

Desertification

In the long term, clearing forests—especially in the tropics—can leave land dry and barren. With lesser forest cover, fewer rain clouds form, wind erodes rich topsoil, and intensive farming strips the ground of nutrients. So the ground is left cracked and baked hard under the sun. This is called desertification.

Moisture evaporates from trees and helps form rain clouds.

Heat bakes the soil into a hard crust.

Livestock trample the soil.

Forest fragmentation

Roads and railroads are often built through forests to connect towns and cities. This carves the habitat into fragments (small parts) and isolates forest animals. Many animals are killed by traffic, and they also avoid crossing open spaces, so it becomes difficult for them to find mates and breed.

Atmospheric pollution

Trees and other plants are sensitive to harmful chemicals in the air. Many of these pollutants, such as sulfur dioxide and other toxic gases, are waste products of factories. These combine with moisture in the air to produce acid rain, which weakens plants and damages their leaves.

Global warming

Burning fossil fuels releases carbon dioxide, and livestock produce methane as they digest food. These greenhouse gases trap heat and warm the planet—a process called global warming. This is shrinking cold-adapted forests and turning tropical forests to drier grasslands and deserts.

The South China tiger is in critical danger of becoming extinct and hasn't been seen in the wild for decades.

Species loss

More species of plants and animals live in forests than in any other land habitat, so destroying forests also means losing much of this biodiversity. The tropics, which have the richest forests of all, are experiencing the greatest loss.

Saving forests

Forests are protected by setting up reserves and national parks, where trees and other wildlife are safeguarded by law. Countries also work together through international agreements to reduce global threats, such as pollution and global warming.

Once barren, Saihanba in China was transformed into a forest by three generations of people through the planting of large numbers of trees, called afforestation.

Cold northern forests

Some of Earth's coldest places also grow the world's largest forests. Vast stretches of evergreen conifers encircle the polar Arctic, spanning the northernmost parts of North America, Europe, and Asia. These forests have cool summers and bitterly cold winters—when snow blankets the leaves and the ground freezes solid beneath the roots.

FACT FILE

Area
1.2 million miles^2
(3.2 million km^2)

Average rainfall
27.5 in (700 mm) annually

Average temperature
5°F (-15°C) winter
to 46°F (8°C) summer

Canadian Shield taiga

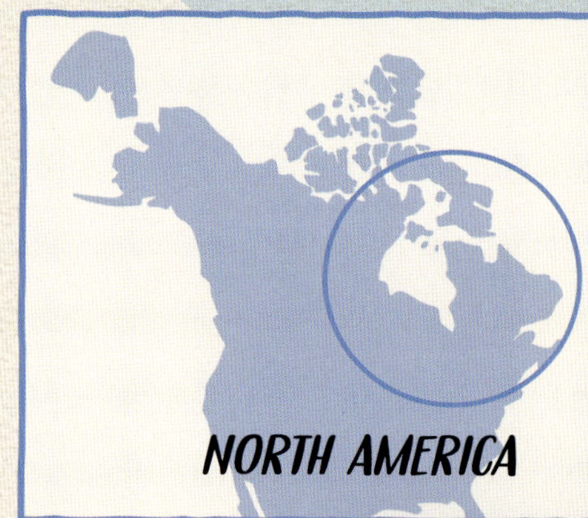

Across Canada's rocky "shield" and wrapped around North America's largest bay lies a sweeping realm of evergreen wilderness.

This forest, called the taiga, is dominated by coniferous spruce trees. It's a landscape of contrasts—closely packed "Christmas trees" stretch far and wide, and wetlands flood the low-lying bedrock where water cannot seep away. This forest is part of the continent's far-northern wilderness.

Wetlands

Trees cannot grow on the wettest lands around Hudson Bay, so grasses, sedges, and floating moss cover the open spaces. These areas, called wetlands, are an important habitat for waterfowl and other birds that visit the nearby forest.

Northern boundary

Conditions get colder closer to the Arctic, where the ground stays frozen year-round. This frozen land, called permafrost, prevents tree growth and marks the northernmost limit of the taiga forest. Beyond it lies the Arctic tundra—a cold, icy habitat that's largely treeless and sparse.

THE CANADIAN SHIELD COVERS NEARLY HALF OF THE COUNTRY'S TOTAL AREA.

Southern transition

At the southern edge of the taiga forest, coniferous spruce trees give way to deciduous broad-leaved trees like aspen. Here, the warmer summers and milder winters mean that temperate broad-leaved forests can grow better than the conifers of the colder taiga.

Geography of the Canadian Shield taiga

The Canadian Shield is a huge slab of rock that sits under North America and is more than 3 billion years old—almost as ancient as Earth itself. But it supports one of the world's youngest forests—a coniferous evergreen taiga that began growing after the last ice age, and spread across the land in just 20,000 years.

Rocky land

The hard granite of the Canadian Shield forms the rocky core of North America. A thin layer of soil lies above it, where a forest of hardy conifers grows. But in some places, the bare granite rock is exposed or lies hidden beneath lakes, bogs, and wetlands.

Icy world

Taiga forest grows close to the polar Arctic, where summers are just warm enough to thaw a thin layer of the ground surface. Further north, the ice is permanent and the ground remains frozen all year round. This layer of underground ice is called permafrost, and it prevents tall trees with deep roots from growing.

Fragments of permafrost can persist under the taiga forest.

Permafrost is continuous under the tundra, so deep roots cannot grow.

Peatland formation

In still pools, dead plants begin to build up, trapped by underground rock and ice. Over thousands of years, this plant matter slowly decays in the cold, waterlogged conditions forming a dark, spongy material called peat. Taiga forests across the northern hemisphere produce much of the world's peatland.

Water-logged lowland

Fallen plants sink to the bottom of the water.

Mats of living sphagnum moss form a layer on the water's surface.

Dead plants collect around the margins and block drainage.

Plant material builds and turns into peat.

Hudson Bay Lowlands

The Hudson Bay is a large saltwater body that stretches more than 621.4 miles (1,000 km) south from the Arctic Ocean, with taiga forest extending around it. Between the shoreline and the forest is a vast network of low-lying wetlands, where more than 20 freshwater rivers drain into the bay.

The rising shield

During the last ice age, the Canadian Shield was covered by a huge ice sheet. The weight of the ice pushed the land down, making it sink lower. When the ice melted, the land began to rise slowly back to its original level. But the Shield is still rising, gradually lifting low-lying wetlands to elevations where coniferous forests grow.

A forest with tall trees is the final mature habitat.

Woody shrubs and tall trees grow on the rising, drier land.

Low wetland has sedges and other short nonwoody plants.

Black spruce

(Picea mariana)

As the most abundant conifer, the black spruce grows well on the wetter ground of the Canadian taiga. This tree has a conical, spirelike shape, and its cones are blue-black in color. The white spruce replaces this species on higher, drier ground farther away from wetlands.

Plants of the Canadian Shield taiga

Forests of the Canadian Shield taiga are defined by just a few species of evergreen conifers. However, a wide variety of shorter plants flourish in the different kinds of open habitats found across this cold northern landscape. Many of these plants are the same or similar to those found in the taiga forests of northern Europe and Asia.

Reindeer lichen

(Cladonia rangiferina)

Lichens are fungi that live in close partnership with algae, helping each other survive. Most lichens form thin crusts on tree bark or rocks. However, the reindeer lichen, named after the caribou that graze on it, grow in thick mats in the ground.

Cloudberry

(Rubus chamaemorus)

Low to the ground, this plant grows in the Arctic tundra but is equally at home in taiga forest clearings. Its tangy fruit, which looks like a golden-yellow version of a blackberry, is a favorite food of bears and other animals.

Its small, round leaves change color in fall, ranging from orange to light red.

Dwarf birch

(Betula nana)

In the Arctic, the creeping dwarf birch rarely grows higher than your boots. However, in the open spaces of the taiga, it is a taller, branching shrub. Like many other cold-adapted plants, it has built-in antifreeze chemicals to help it survive freezing temperatures.

With many light, dainty branches, this lichen grows in soft, cushion-like tufts.

Wetland plants

Plants need to be specially equipped to grow in waterlogged soil, which is low in oxygen and minerals. Sedges, like tussock, and other wetland plants tolerate these tough conditions, but the purple pitcher plant goes a step further—it traps insects and digests them to get extra nutrition.

Taiga alpine
(Erebia mancinus)

Caterpillars of the taiga alpine butterfly feed on the sedges that grow in bogs and marshes. The adult butterflies don't feed at all, so they live for only a few weeks—unlike most other butterflies that are nourished by nectar.

Animals of the Canadian Shield taiga

Many types of animals, such as wolverines, caribou, and moose, are found throughout the vast taiga that stretches across North America, Europe, and Asia. Others, such as garter snakes and wood frogs, are restricted to the North American continent. But all have ways of surviving the cold and making a living in this frozen habitat.

White-winged crossbill
(Loxia leucoptera)

Many birds eat conifer seeds, but crossbills are specially adapted to extract them from cones. Their bill tips cross over, helping them pry open the cone scales, so they can tease out the seeds with their tongues.

Wolverine
(Gulo gulo)

The wolverine is a member of the badger-weasel family. Barely bigger than a medium-sized dog, it has the strength to bring down a moose—the world's largest deer. It hunts for prey and scavenges, feeding on anything it can find.

Their sharp sense of smell allows them to detect prey 20 ft (6 m) under the snow.

Wood frogs stop breathing completely while frozen.

Wood frog

(Lithobates sylvaticus)

This amphibian has a remarkable way of surviving the bitter taiga winters. It hibernates among dead leaves and can survive being partially frozen. It thaws in the springtime melt and breeds quickly in woodland pools in this brief warm spell.

Spruce grouse

(Canachites canadensis)

Members of the grouse family are among the few birds that can digest tough conifer needles. In winter, spruce grouse perch in branches to browse, and in summer, they expand their diet to include fruit and insects.

The red-sided garter snake has three yellow stripes on its body.

Red-sided garter snake

(Thamnophis sirtalis parietalis)

These garter snakes hibernate for eight months of the year in underground dens to avoid freezing. They huddle in huge groups to share body heat, then emerge in spring—sometimes in tens of thousands.

Cape May warbler

This songbird forages for food on the ground.

Connecticut warbler

Swainson's thrush

These thrushes often fly through the night during their seasonal migration.

Migratory birds

Insect-eating birds that breed in the taiga summers include warblers and thrushes. While some seedeaters can find enough food to stay through the winter, others, along with the insect eaters, must fly south to spend the colder months in the milder temperate forests of the US.

Caribou

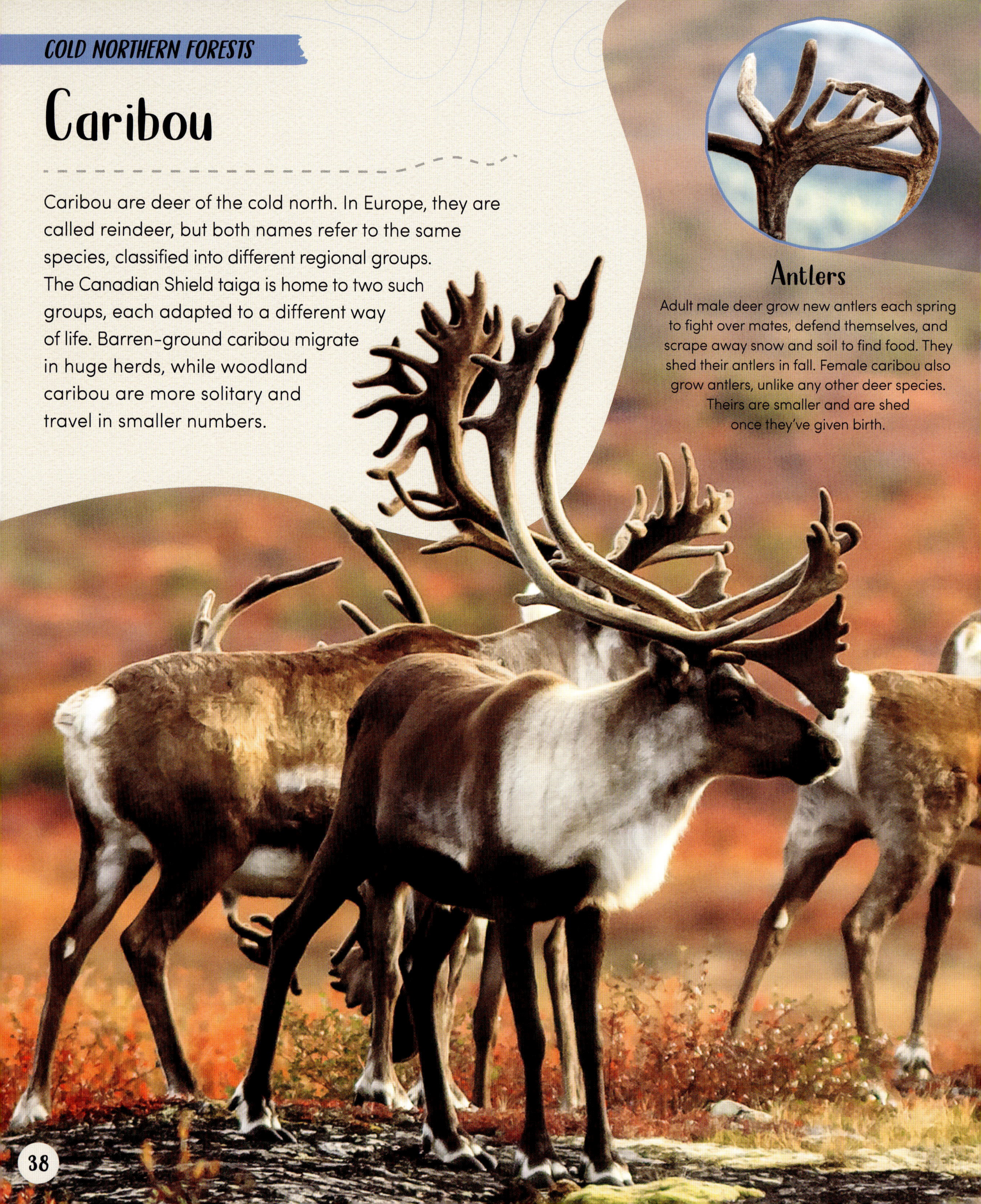

Caribou are deer of the cold north. In Europe, they are called reindeer, but both names refer to the same species, classified into different regional groups. The Canadian Shield taiga is home to two such groups, each adapted to a different way of life. Barren-ground caribou migrate in huge herds, while woodland caribou are more solitary and travel in smaller numbers.

Antlers

Adult male deer grow new antlers each spring to fight over mates, defend themselves, and scrape away snow and soil to find food. They shed their antlers in fall. Female caribou also grow antlers, unlike any other deer species. Theirs are smaller and are shed once they've given birth.

Different habitats

Barren-ground caribou live mostly in the Arctic tundra, moving closer to forests briefly during winter. Woodland caribou are true forest dwellers, living in smaller herds and rarely migrating. In the taiga, they browse on lichen that grows on tree branches and on the ground in clearings.

Woodland caribou are larger and darker than barren-ground caribou.

A female woodland caribou nurses her calf for about two months, after which the calf joins the herd.

Caribou calves

In the Arctic, barren-ground caribou give birth in June, when the lichen crop is at its best. With so many young around, it's harder for wolves to catch each one, so caribou calves are a little safer. Woodland caribou, on the other hand, have a calving season that extends through spring and summer.

Canadian boreal forests

The taiga (boreal) forest of the far north—across America, Europe, and Asia—covers more land area than any other forest on Earth. Snow blankets this habitat for much of the year. Most of the conifer trees that grow here keep their leaves through the long winters, even though photosynthesis and other life processes slow down almost to a stop.

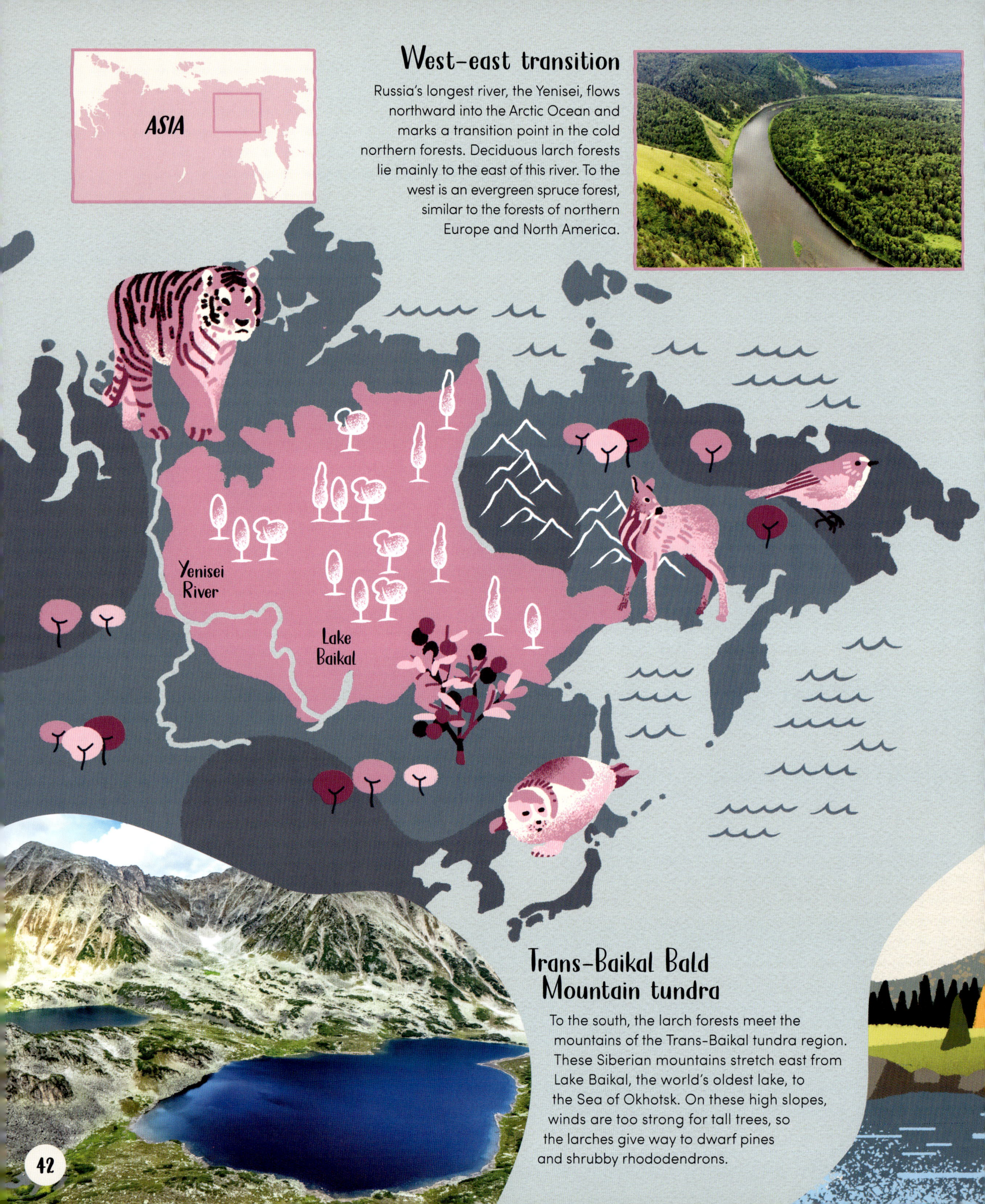

West-east transition

Russia's longest river, the Yenisei, flows northward into the Arctic Ocean and marks a transition point in the cold northern forests. Deciduous larch forests lie mainly to the east of this river. To the west is an evergreen spruce forest, similar to the forests of northern Europe and North America.

Trans-Baikal Bald Mountain tundra

To the south, the larch forests meet the mountains of the Trans-Baikal tundra region. These Siberian mountains stretch east from Lake Baikal, the world's oldest lake, to the Sea of Okhotsk. On these high slopes, winds are too strong for tall trees, so the larches give way to dwarf pines and shrubby rhododendrons.

East Siberian larch forests

The world's coldest forests extend from the middle of Siberia eastward as far as the Pacific.

Winter temperatures in Siberia can drop lower than in parts of Antarctica. Conditions are so extreme that even the hardy conifers cannot keep their leaves all year round. Instead, Siberia's larch trees turn golden in fall before dropping their needles onto the snowy ground, leaving winter branches bare and bleak.

FACT FILE

Area
772,204 miles^2
(2 million km^2)

Average rainfall
12.6in (322mm) annually

Average temperature
-35°F (-37°C) winter
to 61°F (16°C) summer

Siberian larch needles are usually about 0.8–1.2 in (2–3 cm) long.

Larch forests

East Siberian larch forests grow in a region with permafrost all year round, even in summers. These are among the largest forests with deciduous conifers. Siberian larch grows in the west and south, and Dahurian larch in the north and east. Where their ranges meet, the trees mix and grow together.

Geography of the east Siberian larch forests

Siberia's larch forests lie close to the polar Arctic, like other great northern conifer forests. But east Siberia is extra icy, locked deep within the giant continent of Asia. It's far from the ocean, so there's nothing to keep the climate mild. The cold arrives and stays for most of the year.

Vegetation mosaic

Much of the Siberian taiga is made up of a single species of larch. As summer shifts into fall, green leaves turn yellow before dropping altogether. Patches of low, treeless tundra vegetation are scattered through the forest, creating a mix of these hardy plants and trees.

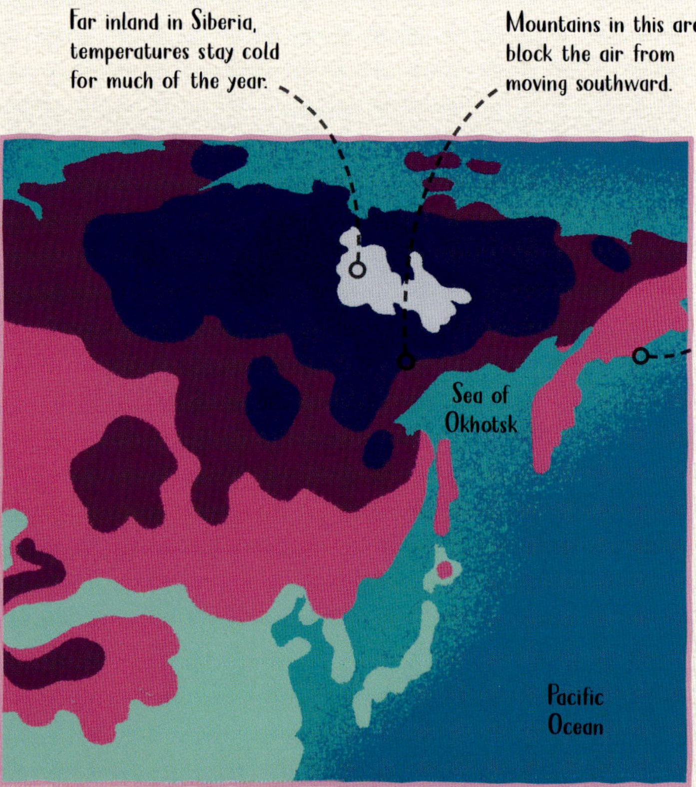

Matching heights

Larches growing in the same place tend to have similar heights because they age together. As old trees fall, new ones sprout quickly from the seeds buried under the bare ground. The tallest grow to 148 ft (45 m).

Trapping the cold

Weather changes as wind blows and air circulates, spreading the sun's warmth. But in Siberia, winter air becomes trapped between the Arctic to the north and mountains to the south. It then stagnates, causing temperatures to plunge to -40°F (-40°C).

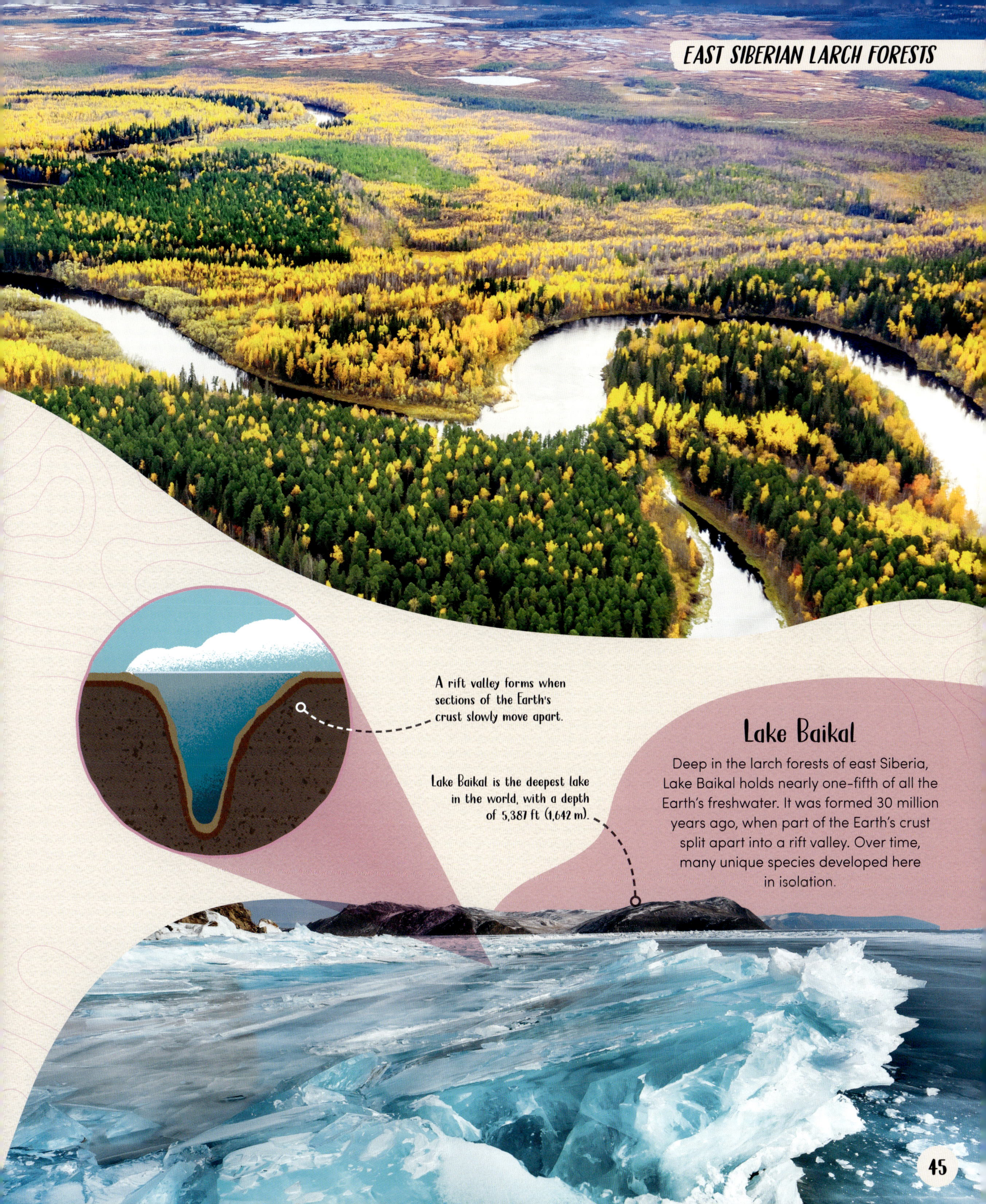

Lake Baikal

Deep in the larch forests of east Siberia, Lake Baikal holds nearly one-fifth of all the Earth's freshwater. It was formed 30 million years ago, when part of the Earth's crust split apart into a rift valley. Over time, many unique species developed here in isolation.

Plants of the east Siberian larch forests

Siberia's seasonal plant life transforms the larch forests into landscapes of shifting color. Larches turn from leafy green in summer to golden yellow in fall—just as bushes blush with vibrant red berries. A long winter of white snow and ice follows, before flowers bloom again in spring.

Siberian larch
(Larix sibirica)

This larch species dominates the cold forests across much of central and eastern Siberia. Like all larches, it has green needle leaves that grow in fanlike clusters. These turn yellow in fall before shedding off for the long, freezing winter.

Its bright yellow cap turns a burnt orange as the mushroom grows.

Siberian larch bolete
(Suillus grevillei)

The fall of larch leaves nourishes fungi like the Siberian larch bolete, helping it grow spore-producing mushrooms. The bolete and the larch roots also share nutrients in a special partnership called mycorrhiza.

Lingonberry
(Vaccinium vitis-idaea)

Bare winter branches of larch trees allow sunlight to reach evergreen shrubs growing beneath them. Among them is the lingonberry, tough enough to survive subzero temperatures. Its summer flowers provide nectar for bees, while its fall berries offer food to birds and mammals.

Siberian rhododendron
(Rhododendron dauricum)

Cold-tolerant rhododendrons are among the most common shrubs in the larch forests. They start flowering early in the year, giving insects enough time to pollinate their blooms and allowing seeds to develop during Siberia's brief summer.

Alpine sedge
(Carex nivalis)

Low-lying parts of Siberia, where drainage is poor, gather water that thaws only during the short summer. These wetland habitats host ice-tolerant plants, such as alpine sedge and grasses, which thrive in open areas away from the shade of larch trees.

Cold-adapted larch

Conifers are built to survive extremes, and larches are among the hardiest of them all. Their needlelike leaves help many conifers endure drought or freezing cold. Most types of conifers can keep growing under the worst conditions and stay green all year. But larches are deciduous—they drop their leaves to help them withstand some of the most severe winters on Earth.

Needle leaves

The needle-shaped leaves of conifers have a waxy coating and a core packed with antifreeze resin. These features help trap water inside and stop the trees from freezing solid when temperatures drop below zero.

Coping with snow

Heavy snowfall can damage trees by weighing down their branches and blocking the light from reaching the leaves. The conical Christmas-tree shape of larches and other conifers helps snow slide off, preventing it from piling up and causing harm.

Winter leaf loss

Most conifers keep their leaves through the dark winter, so they're ready to take advantage of spring sunshine without having to grow new ones. But Siberian winters are too cold even for conifers, so larches shed their leaves. But once the weather turns warmer, they grow them back very quickly.

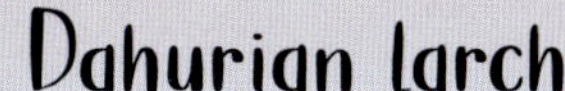

Dahurian larch

The Siberian larch is the dominant tree across the region, but closer to the Arctic grows a second species—the Dahurian larch. With a darker bark and extreme cold tolerance, it is the world's most northerly tree.

Animals of the east Siberian larch forests

Animals of east Siberia have special characteristics that help them survive in these frosty larch forests. Most do not stay through the bleak, exposed winter and migrate elsewhere. Others prefer to live at the edges of these forests, where there is more food. However, a few hardy species make their home here all year round.

The larch sawfly larvae have a gray-green body with a white underside.

Larch sawfly

(Pristiphora erichsonii)

Sawflies spend the Siberian winter in cocoons, buried underground. In spring, the adults break out to fly and feed on pollen or nectar, then lay eggs in larch shoots. The eggs hatch into caterpillar-like larvae that eat larch leaves.

Its bronze-brown color helps it blend well into the barren landscape.

Siberian salamander

(Salamandrella keyserlingii)

Few amphibians live as far north as the Siberian salamander. It goes to extreme lengths to survive here all year—hibernating under frozen ground and staying inactive in a shrunken state for years.

Siberian tiger

(Panthera tigris altaica)

Siberian tigers are the world's largest big cats. Unlike smaller animals, their huge size helps them hold body heat better and stay warm in the cold larch forests. These large predators need lots of food, so they mostly stay near the forest borders where prey is easier to find.

Red-flanked bluetail

(Tarsiger cyanurus)

This bird nests in tree hollows during the Siberian summer, feeding its chicks on insects. But like many insect-eating birds of these larch forests, it flies south when the food runs out, spending winter in the tropics of Southeast Asia.

Siberian musk deer

(Moschus moschiferus)

This small fang-toothed deer is one of the few mammals that can live throughout the year in Siberia's larch forests. It survives the winter by mostly eating lichen, which grows abundantly—especially on higher ground and in clearings.

Baikal seal

(Pusa sibirica)

The world's only freshwater seal evolved from marine seals that once lived in the Arctic. It is thought that these ancient seals reached Lake Baikal long ago, when it was connected to the Arctic Ocean by rivers or seaways.

Blakiston's fish owl

(Ketupa blakistoni)

This is one of the largest owls in the world. It nests in the tops of larch trees near rivers and lakes, where there's plenty of prey. Blakiston's fish owl swoops low over the water or wades into the shallows to grab fish with its talons.

Surviving winter

Many animals that once roamed the harsh, frozen Arctic ventured south to the Siberian taiga in search of a gentler habitat. Used to life on the open polar tundra, the Arctic fox is equally at home among the snow-covered trees of the taiga. It hunts small rodents, relying on its white winter coat for camouflage and sharp hearing to detect prey burrowing beneath the snow.

Temperate forests

The world's temperate zones lie between the frigid polar regions and the equatorial tropics. The temperate forests are strongly influenced by the shifting seasons—from sunny summers to snowy winters. In the northern hemisphere, temperate trees include broad-leaved oaks and beeches that lose their leaves. In the southern hemisphere, the forests have many evergreens. Some of the richest temperate forests are found in North America and eastern Asia.

FACT FILE

Area
5,255 miles² (13,610 km²)

Average rainfall
63 in (1,600 mm) annually

Average temperature
39°F (4°C) winter
to 57°F (14°C) summer

Californian redwood forests

Clinging to the misty Pacific, these redwood forests are a rich realm of conifers that grow along the rugged coasts and deep valleys of California.

Along North America's Pacific west side, conifer trees grow into giants in California's temperate forests. Here, the coast redwoods—the world's tallest trees—tower above a forest floor carpeted by ferns. Heavy winter rains and summer fogs from the Pacific Ocean nourish this lush world, creating one of Earth's richest habitats.

Visitors from the sea

Being close to the Pacific Ocean, the redwood forests receive some unlikely seagoing visitors. These include the marbled murrelet, a bird related to puffins, that nests in redwood treetops.

Murrelets zoom over the ocean to catch fish—sometimes even up to 3 miles (5 km) from the shoreline.

Giant trees

Coast redwoods can rise as tall as a 22-story building, or four times the height of a mature oak tree. The tallest tree in the world, named Hyperion, reaches 381 ft (116 m) high and grows deep in the forests of California.

Redwood National Parks

Nearly half of the coast redwood forests are protected within four US national parks, where habitats and tourism are managed. These rich coniferous rainforests, which are home to several record-breaking giant trees, were named a United Nations World Heritage Site in 1980.

Geography of the Californian redwood forests

Fossils show that more than 10 million years ago, many different types of redwood trees were widespread across the northern hemisphere. Today, only a few species remain, found mainly in forests in western North America and China. The last ice age killed most of them, but survivors, like the coast redwood, clung on along the wet, mild coastlines and sheltered valleys of California.

Fog and rain

The western coast of North America receives heavy rain clouds from the Pacific Ocean during the long, wet winter, from October to May. In summer, cool ocean air condenses over the warmer land, forming thick fog that envelops the forest canopy.

Sierra Nevada rain shadow

Along the Sierra Nevada mountain range in western North America, high mountains catch moist winds driven inland from the ocean. This creates a "rain shadow"—a dry region on the far side of the mountains—while rain falls heavily on the Pacific-facing forests.

Fire cycle

Although redwood forests are damp, they still experience occasional fires, especially during summers in the drier south. Ocean winds can help ignite tinder, but redwoods often survive to regrow. Fire can also create clearings where new trees grow from seeds.

Petrified Forest

California's Petrified Forest holds striking fossil evidence that redwood trees once grew far inland. The stony remains of giant redwood trunks show that the forest was destroyed by an eruption of the Mount Saint Helens volcano 3.4 million years ago.

Plants of the Californian redwood forests

With lofty trunks as wide as a bus and branches draped with wet moss, California's coastal redwoods make up a rich temperate rainforest. Like tropical rainforests, plant life flourishes both on the forest floor and high up in the trees. Vegetation is lush and evergreen—from the needle leaves high in the canopy to ferns unfurling below.

Slender mouse-tail moss

(Isothecium myosuroides)

Rain and fog keep the tall redwood branches damp for days, creating the perfect home for mosses. Slender mouse-tail moss is one of hundreds of species of epiphytes—plants that grow perched on tree bark, absorbing nutrients from fallen leaves.

Coast live oak

(Quercus agrifolia)

In California, winters are mild so oak trees here stay evergreen, just like the conifers. One of these is the coast live oak, a species native to California and Central America. It can even tolerate salt blown in from the sea.

Coast live oaks can live for centuries, often surviving more than 250 years.

Evergreen huckleberry

(Vaccinium ovatum)

In the deep shade beneath the canopy of giant redwoods, evergreen huckleberry thrives. A cousin of deciduous huckleberries found further inland, this is a dominant shrub in the Pacific temperate rainforests.

The berries are said to be the sweetest after the first frost of winter.

Douglas fir

(Pseudotsuga menziesii)

The tallest tree in the pine–fir family, the Douglas fir grows well on higher, drier slopes of the Pacific Coast. Though not as massive as redwoods, mature Douglas firs can still rise to twice the height of northern pines and larches.

Coast redwood

(Sequoia sempervirens)

Mature coast redwoods have huge trunks that stretch straight up for more than 230 ft (70 m). They branch into leafy crowns that can exceed a total height of 367 ft (112 m). Their bark is thick, soft, and fibrous, with a red-brown color that gives the tree its name.

Western sword fern

(Polystichum munitum)

The most abundant fern of the Pacific rainforest, this species blankets the forest floor with its arching divided leaves. Like other ferns and mosses, it reproduces by spores that drift through the air and germinate on wet ground.

Redwood life cycle

Some coast redwoods are not only the world's tallest trees, but they are also among the oldest—surviving for more than 2,000 years. They are built to last—their roots tolerate flooding and their thick bark absorbs moisture directly from the coastal fog. The lofty trunks of the trees keep leaves high above the ground—away from forest fires that start down below.

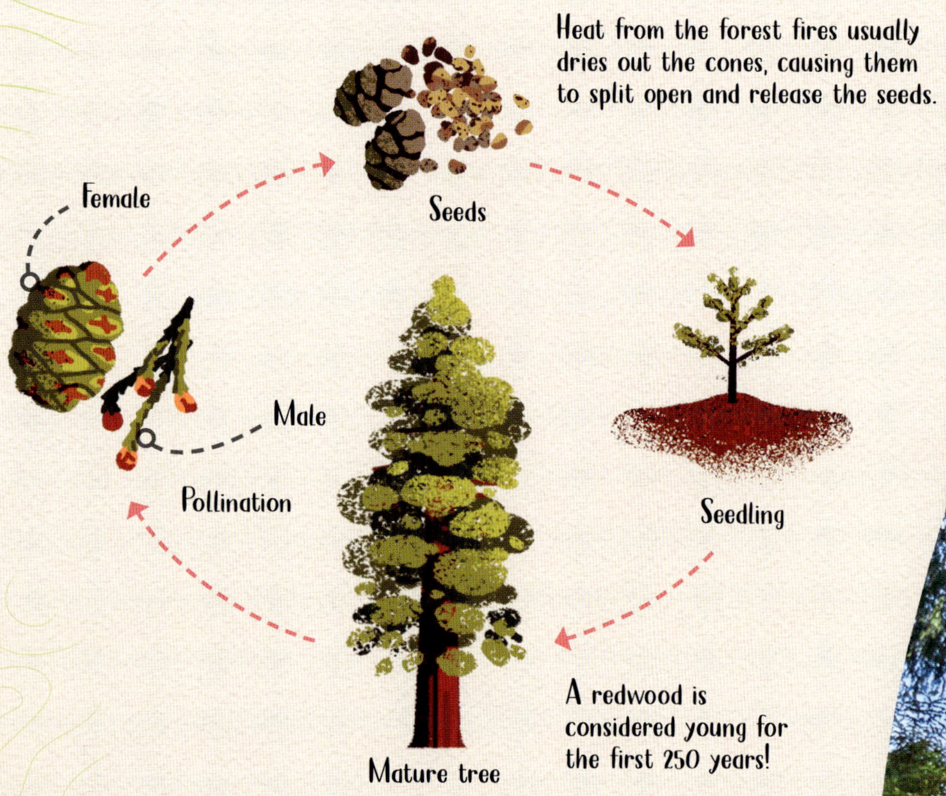

Heat from the forest fires usually dries out the cones, causing them to split open and release the seeds.

Seeds

Female

Male

Pollination

Seedling

Mature tree

A redwood is considered young for the first 250 years!

Life cycle

Coast redwoods start reproducing at around 10 years old, with each tree bearing both male and female cones. In late winter, male cones release pollen that is blown on the wind to female cones, fertilizing their eggs so seeds can form. The seeds take nearly a year to develop, and scatter on the ground when female cones open the following winter. These seeds sprout best in ash-rich soil after forest fires.

Lignotubers

Trees damaged by fire or wind can regenerate using swollen growths, called lignotubers, near the base of their trunks. These structures help cambium, a growth tissue in the bark, to form new shoots. Over time, the shoots can grow to replace dead or damaged trunks.

Goosepens

Hollow openings can sometimes form in big redwood trees when they are struck by fire or crushed by falling neighboring trees. Early European settlers kept geese and other fowl in these hollows, earning them the name "goosepens." Despite the damage, the trees survive because their living tissue is confined to the outermost layers of the trunk, which remain unharmed.

Western skink
(Plestiodon skiltonianus)

Sun-basking reptiles typically avoid cool, wet forests, but lizards such as the western skink can be common in warmer clearings. They are more easily spotted on open land where redwood forests regrow after wildfires.

If threatened, it detaches its bright blue tail to distract predators and escape.

Red tree vole
(Arborimus longicaudus)

This little rodent spends its entire life in the canopy of Douglas firs. It nibbles on the soft outer coat of the needles, leaving behind the tough, sticky core. The vole then uses the leftover cores to build its treetop nest.

Animals of the Californian redwood forests

The tallest redwood rainforests provide multistoried habitats for animals. Some spend their entire lives in the lofty canopy, while others stick closer to the ground. The thick forest provides shelter all year round for many animals. But there are also seasonal visitors, migrating here from faraway forests, or even coming inland from the open ocean.

Varied thrush
(Ixoreus naevius)

The varied thrush is a bird of the Pacific coastal forests, which stretch from California to Alaska in the US. In summer, it breeds in cooler forests as far north as Alaska. Then it migrates south to California, where it feeds on winter berries growing in the shade of the redwood trees.

This skydiving salamander can go its entire life without ever touching the ground.

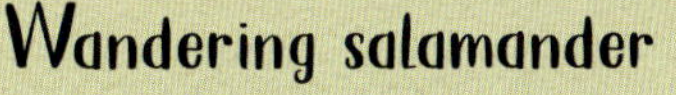

Wandering salamander

(Aneides vagrans)

Wet redwood forests are the perfect habitat for moist-skinned amphibians like the wandering salamander. One of many lungless species, it breathes only through its skin. It climbs in high canopy, leaping from branch to branch to escape predators.

As an adult, this millipede can reach a length of up to 2 in (5 cm).

Marbled murrelet

(Brachyramphus marmoratus)

Most seabirds nest on clifftops or in burrows, but the marbled murrelet raises its young in redwood trees. It lays a single egg on a soft bed of moss and lichen. Parents fly in from the Pacific Ocean at dawn and dusk with fish for the young.

Yellow-spotted millipede

(Harpaphe haydeniana)

Thick vegetation produces lots of dead leaves that fall to the ground, becoming food for tiny invertebrates such as this millipede. Its striking colors warn other animals that it is laced with a poisonous chemical, called cyanide, for defense.

After about a month, the chick leaves the nest and flies to the ocean alone.

American black bear

As the seasons change in the redwood valleys, so does the menu for hungry forest animals. The American black bear makes the most of it. In summer, it eats more meat and eggs, feeding on newborn fawns and raiding bird nests. As the year passes and fall cools the forest, the bear turns to the trees laden with fruit and berries.

Area
121,684 miles^2 (315,159 km^2)

Average rainfall
35 in (900 mm) annually

Average temperature
39°F (4°C) winter
to 61°F (16°C) summer

BRITISH OAKS SUPPORT NEARLY 300 SPECIES OF INSECTS.

British oak-beech forests

Ancient oaks and lowland beeches form the heart of the natural forest habitat of the British Isles (mainly Great Britain and Ireland).

The cycle of seasons—warm summers and cold winters—shapes the temperate broad-leaved forest. In Britain and continental Europe, these forests are dominated by oaks and beeches, which can live for centuries and shed their leaves each fall. This is a place where all the plants and animals work to their calendar, from springtime flowers to migrating birds.

Scottish Highlands

At higher altitudes in the Scottish Highlands, oaks and beeches give way to cool-adapted birches and conifers. Northern birds such as bramblings mostly visit the lowlands in winter, but they may stay back all year in these highland woods.

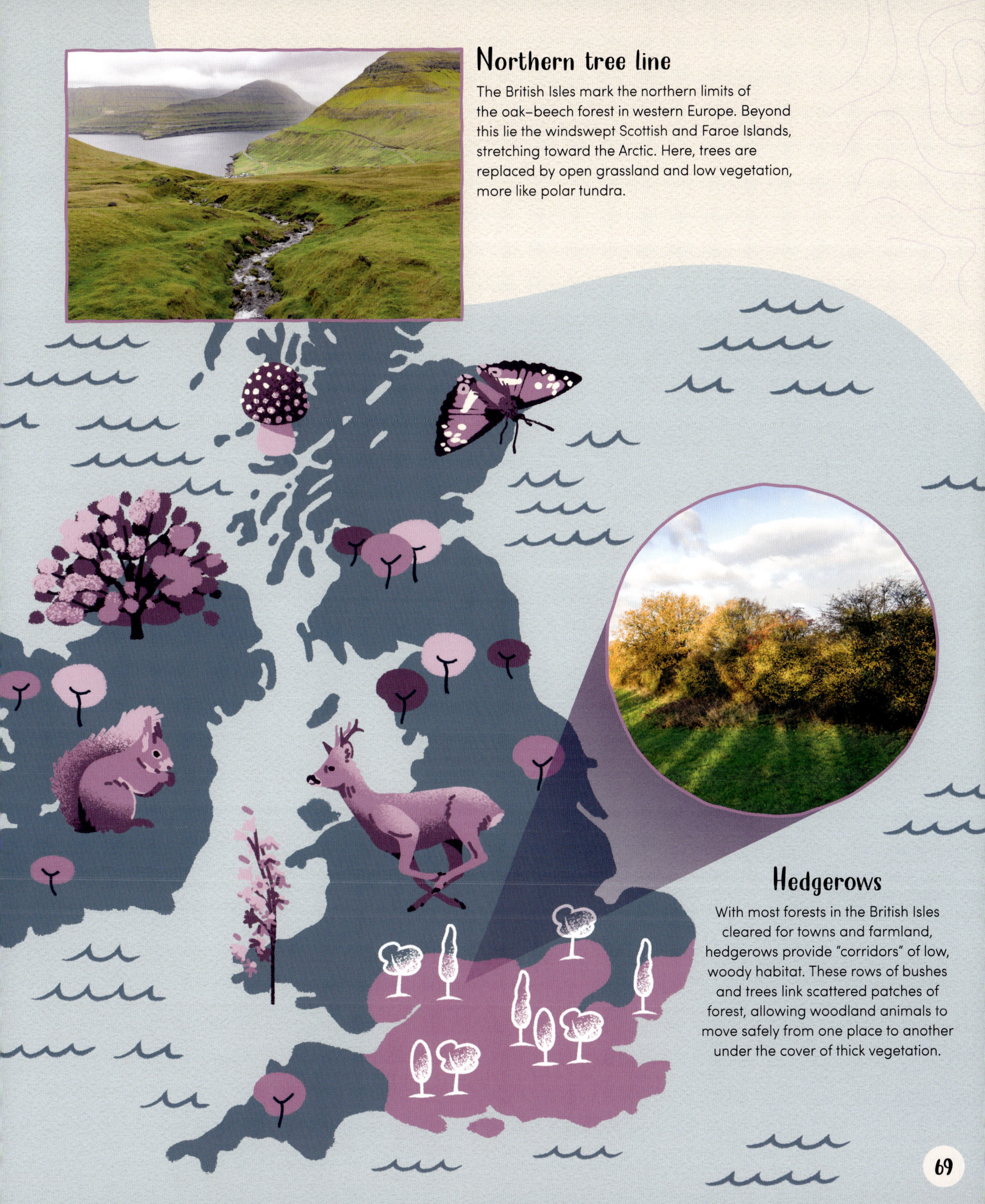

Northern tree line

The British Isles mark the northern limits of the oak–beech forest in western Europe. Beyond this lie the windswept Scottish and Faroe Islands, stretching toward the Arctic. Here, trees are replaced by open grassland and low vegetation, more like polar tundra.

Hedgerows

With most forests in the British Isles cleared for towns and farmland, hedgerows provide "corridors" of low, woody habitat. These rows of bushes and trees link scattered patches of forest, allowing woodland animals to move safely from one place to another under the cover of thick vegetation.

The Gulf Stream is one of the strongest ocean currents.

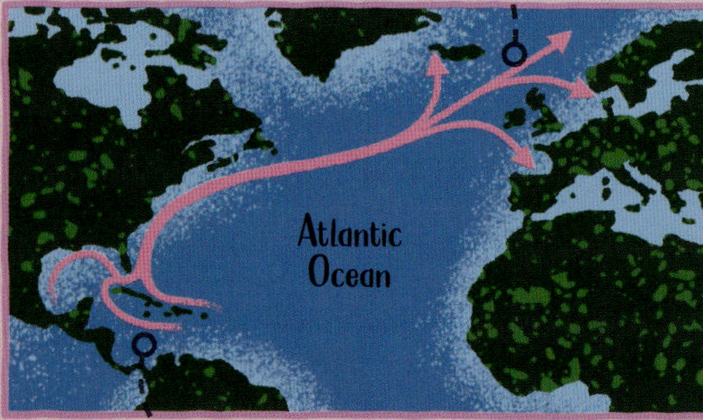

Water warmed by the sun flows out from the Gulf of Mexico.

Gulf Stream

An ocean current called the Gulf Stream flows northeast from the tropical Caribbean to the British Isles, nearly 5,000 miles (8,000 km) away. It brings warmth to the region, making winters less harsh. Forests grow well, even forming temperate oak rainforests along the western coasts.

Geography of the British oak-beech forests

Before humans settled in the British Isles about 80,000 years ago, vast forests almost completely covered the land. These forests were mostly made up of two tree species—the pedunculate oak and the common beech. Warmed by ocean currents coming from the tropical Atlantic, the islands' mild climate allows the trees to flourish and extend further north here than in the rest of Europe and Asia.

English lowlands

In the British Isles, forests of common beeches grow in southern England, where porous rocks create well-drained soil. Each spring, bluebells carpet the forest floor, painting it in rich purples and blues. In chalk-rich areas, soil is more alkaline, favoring ash and whitebeam trees.

Moorland and meadows

Thousands of years of livestock farming have deforested much of Britain. Moorland now covers the upland, peat-rich regions of Scotland, while the chalky lowlands of England have meadows. Both are human-made habitats, now home to plants from other regions—such as mountains, bogs, and marshes—elsewhere in Europe.

Oaks or beeches?

The common beech is the most widespread tree in broad-leaved forests across much of continental Europe. But oaks grow across a wider range of climates. The pedunculate oak thrives in the wetter British Isles to the north, while the cork oak prefers the dry Mediterranean region to the south.

Human-made meadows and moorland are created for specific purposes such as pastures for grazing livestock and deer.

Plants of the British oak-beech forests

Most trees of the British lowland forests are deciduous, but some such as holly are evergreen. All these plants bloom during spring or summer. Early spring flowers enjoy more light under bare branches and face less competition for pollinating insects. Summer flowers produce fall fruit that nourish many animals as they prepare for the coldest winter months.

Common beech

(Fagus sylvatica)

In summer, the common beech has dense foliage that casts deep shade, leaving little light for plants to grow beneath. Its fall nuts, called masts, are a vital food source for birds, such as bramblings and chaffinches.

In winter, some trees cling to dry fall leaves—a feature known as marcescence.

Fly agaric

(Amanita muscaria)

Often spotted growing in rings around birches, pines, and beeches, the fly agaric forms mycorrhizal relationships with these trees. Its scientific name comes from the Latin *musca*, meaning "fly", because it was once used to kill flies.

The cap releases reproductive spores from its underside.

Pedunculate oak

(Quercus robur)

Also called the English oak, this tree was once widespread in ancient forests across Britain. Mature trees can live more than 1,000 years, supporting more than 2,000 different animal species, ranging from leaf-eating insects to mammals that feed on their acorns.

The spines on holly leaves help deter leaf-eating animals.

Oak branches and foliage spread over a wide area.

Common holly

(Ilex aquifolium)

Unlike many trees, male and female holly flowers grow on separate plants. The evergreen spiny leaves are shade-tolerant, so hollies are common in the forest understory. Bright red berries last through the winter but are poisonous to many animals.

Multiple flowers hang beneath each drooping stem.

Common bluebell

(Hyacinthoides non-scripta)

In spring, bluebells sprout their leaves from underground bulbs, then produce drooping flowers between April and June. The blooms create a shimmering sea of blue across forest clearings. They attract many species of bees, butterflies, and hoverflies for pollination.

Common ivy

(Hedera helix)

Climbers such as ivy cling to trees and other plants, using them as support to grow upward and reach more light. They produce thickets of woody branches, which offer safe nesting spots for birds.

Ivy leaves have three to five sections or lobes.

Animals of the British oak-beech forests

Many of the animals now native to Britain reached its forests by crossing from mainland Europe when sea levels were low enough for them to walk across. Today, mammals and most invertebrates reside in British woodlands throughout the year, though some hibernate during winter. Birds include seedeaters that stay and feed through the winter, and insect eaters that migrate to warmer regions.

Eurasian goshawk

(Accipiter gentilis)

An agile flier, the Eurasian goshawk is one of the top predators of British forests. It hunts birds the size of pheasants and small mammals such as squirrels. The goshawk soars high above the trees to spot its prey, then darts between the branches to catch it.

Roe deer

(Capreolus capreolus)

The roe deer is one of two native British deer species, along with the larger red deer. It browses on shoots and foliage when plants are in leaf, then switches its diet to include more fruit, acorns, and fungi during fall and winter.

This deer flaunts a distinctive black "mustache."

Eurasian red squirrel

(Sciurus vulgaris)

Once widespread in Britain, the native red squirrel's numbers have declined due to deforestation and competition from gray squirrels introduced from North America. Today, it survives mainly in the coniferous forests of Scotland and Ireland.

Purple emperor

(Apatura iris)

This butterfly lives in the canopy, where it feeds on tree sap and honeydew droplets produced by sap-sucking insects, called aphids. Males have glossy purple wings, while females are brown. They lay eggs on willow trees, where caterpillars hatch and feed on the leaves until they turn into butterflies.

European robin

(Erithacus rubecula)

Most British robins stay in their forest habitats throughout the year. They often build nests in damp, shady places close to the ground. In summer, robins snack on worms, snails, and insects. In winter, they feed on berries, nuts, and seeds to stay full.

Unlike snakes, slow worms and other lizards have eyelids, so they can blink.

Great crested newt

(Triturus cristatus)

This is Britain's largest species of newt. It breeds in ponds and small lakes, where it lays eggs on aquatic plants. The eggs hatch into swimming larvae that grow into walking adults. Once mature, the newts move onto land and hibernate in damp spots in forests and hedgerows.

Common slow worm

(Anguis fragilis)

This animal resembles a snake but is really a legless lizard. Like other reptiles, the slow worm enjoys basking in sunlit clearings. In summer, females give birth to live young. Slow worms are less active in winter, when they hibernate underground.

Brambling

(Fringilla montifringilla)

While most migratory woodland birds fly to Britain during summer, the brambling arrives in winter, after spending its mating season in the colder Scandinavian taiga. It feeds on winter seeds, especially the nuts, or mast, of beech trees.

Eurasian badgers

A familiar animal of English forests, the badger has the densest population in Britain than anywhere else in Europe and Asia. This nocturnal mammal is Britain's largest native carnivore, closely related to weasels and otters. Badgers live in groups in underground burrows and remain active throughout winter.

Badger calendar

Badgers begin mating in spring, but females delay their pregnancy until December, with most cubs born in February. They emerge from their burrows in April or May. Typically active from dusk onward—searching for food or playing—badgers remain underground for longer periods in winter.

Life in a sett

Badgers use their strong, clawed feet to dig extensive burrows, known as setts. Setts can house six or more animals for many years. They contain a network of tunnels that connect sleeping and breeding chambers, lined with soft grass and ferns. The biggest setts can have more than 984 ft (300 m) of tunnels and more than 50 entrances.

Tracks and signs

An entrance to a badger's sett is usually a large hole in a sloping bank. Its low-slung body wears down paths through the vegetation, creating well-trodden trails. One might also spot its paw prints, droppings, or clumps of hair snagged on wire fences.

Droppings

Footprints

Tracks

Newborn cubs

A badger litter can have up to five cubs. They open their eyes at five weeks and nurse on their mother's milk for 12 weeks. All adults in the sett help care for the cubs. The youngsters usually stay in the sett where they were born, but some may leave to find new homes.

Forest floor

Littered with fallen leaves, the forest floor comes alive in fall. Many fungi sprout as toadstools and mushrooms, like these fly agarics. Their vivid red caps, speckled with white, sit atop pale undersides and slender stems. Together, they form the spore-producing fruiting bodies seen above ground. Beneath the forest floor, the shared main body—called the mycelium—spreads as a web of fine threads, drawing nutrients from fallen leaves and decaying waste.

FACT FILE

Area
47,722 miles^2
(123,600 km^2)

Average rainfall
35 in (900 mm)
annually

Average temperature
77°F (25°C) to 18°F (–8°C)

Conservation icon

Giant pandas were once widespread across China's temperate bamboo forests. Today, however, they are found only in remote patches of their natural habitat such as the Qinling. Their growing popularity over the years has helped draw attention to the importance of conserving these forests.

Qinling deciduous forests

As ancient as the dinosaurs, China's Qinling (Qin Mountains) lie at the heart of East Asia's rich temperate forests in central China.

In these deciduous woodlands, giant grasses called bamboo tower over trees, and wild giant pandas—China's iconic animal known worldwide—roam freely. Cloaked in forests since before the last ice age, the mountains have had plenty of time for a rich diversity of plants and animals to evolve.

East Asian forests

East Asia hosts many types of forests. They stretch from the snowy taiga of Siberia through the temperate woodlands of China, Japan, North Korea, and South Korea to tropical forests further south. China's temperate forests are among the world's richest, with an extraordinary diversity of evergreen and deciduous trees.

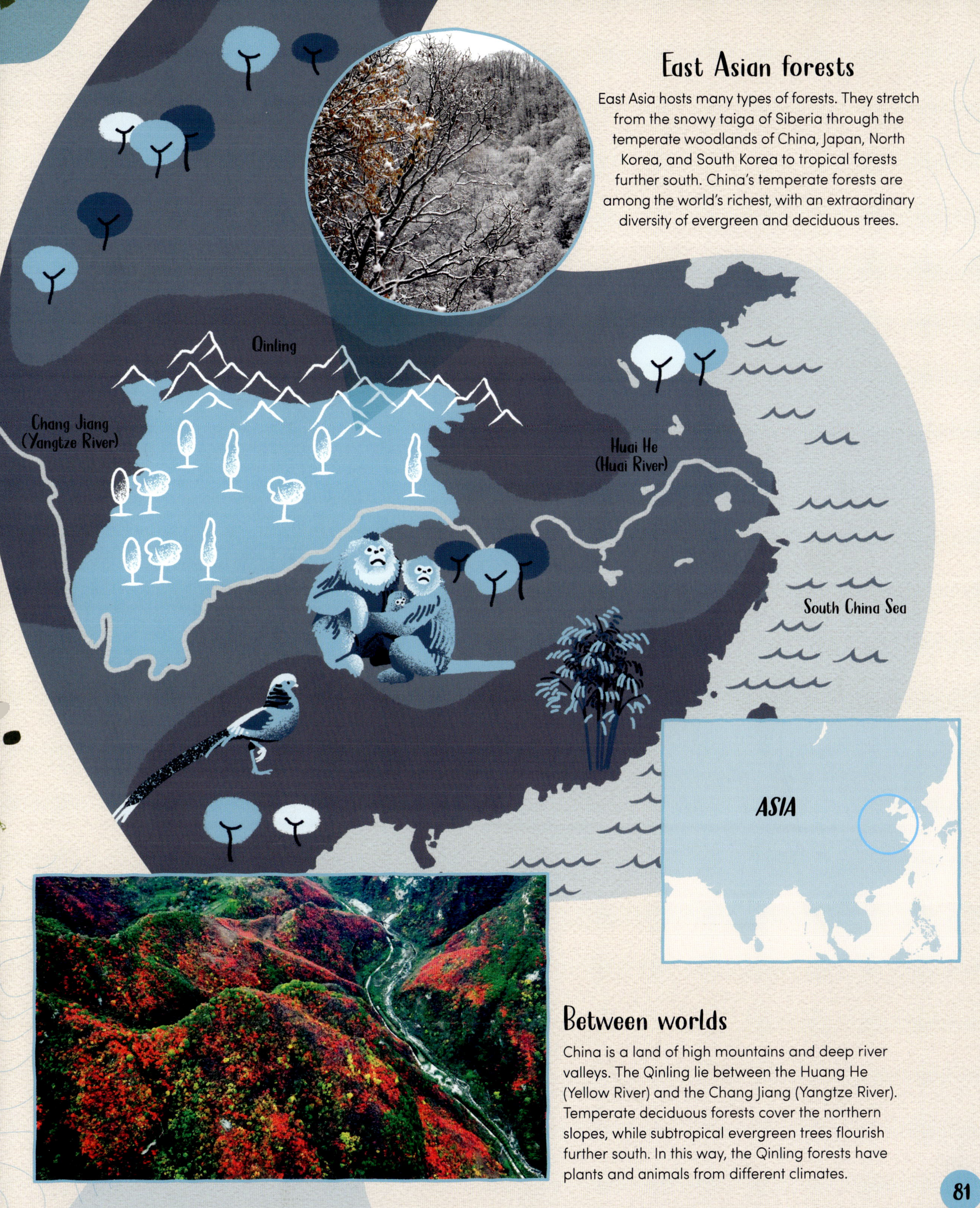

Between worlds

China is a land of high mountains and deep river valleys. The Qinling lie between the Huang He (Yellow River) and the Chang Jiang (Yangtze River). Temperate deciduous forests cover the northern slopes, while subtropical evergreen trees flourish further south. In this way, the Qinling forests have plants and animals from different climates.

Geography of the Qinling deciduous forests

Rising to more than 12,336 ft (3,760 m) on steep peaks, China's Qinling host a unique mix of plants and animals of East Asia. The mountains lie between the cool temperate forests of the north and the subtropical forests of the south. Qinling's rich diversity comes from this overlap of habitats, which takes a share from both worlds, as well as from the region's ancient history.

Ancient origins

The Qinling were formed about 200 million years ago, when the lands were ruled by dinosaurs. At that time, South China existed as a separate continent and struck Asia as it moved westward. This resulted in land being pushed up to form mountains in the collision zone.

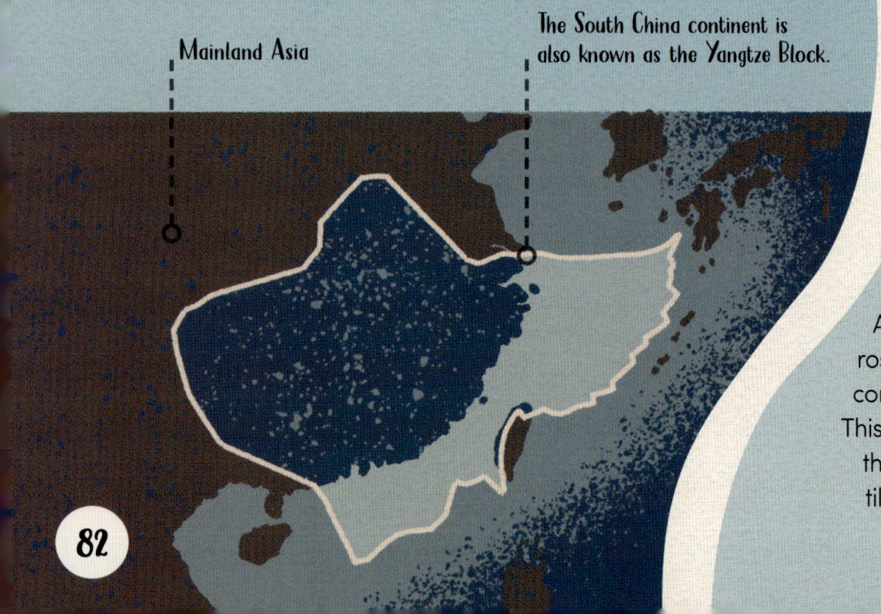

Mainland Asia

The South China continent is also known as the Yangtze Block.

Pushed higher

About 50 million years ago, the Qinling rose even higher when the isolated Indian continent collided with Asia from the south. This created the Himalayas, but also buckled the land of China to the east, folding and tilting it to form Qinling's steepest slopes.

Ice age refuge

About 2.6 million years ago, the last ice age covered much of northern Asia in a thick ice sheet. It killed trees and turned forests into open grassland. But the ice never reached the forests of East Asia—helping to preserve the biodiversity in the Qinling.

Qinling-Huaihe line

The Huai He (Huai River) starts in the Qinling and flows east to the Yellow Sea. Together, the mountain range and the river mark the divide between temperate and subtropical China. In the north, winters are icy cold, while in the south, they are milder.

Plants of the Qinling deciduous forests

Although many trees and shrubs of the Qinling lose their leaves in winter, these forests are mixed—with oaks, elms, and chestnuts growing alongside evergreen conifers. There are more tree species here than in Europe's temperate forests. This is because the giant glaciers of the last ice age never reached this region to wipe out its plant life.

Arrow bamboo

(Fargesia qinlingensis)

Bamboos grow so tall because they have hard, woody tissues, similar to trees. Their narrow, polelike stems are hollow. Arrow bamboo, one of hundreds of species in China, grows in massive clumps and is a top food choice for browsing pandas.

It has long, tapering, grassy leaves.

Peacock orchid

(Pleione sp.)

With over 25,000 species, orchids are one of the largest families of flowering plants, and nearly every habitat has its own unique representatives. Peacock orchids, named for their colorful blooms, grow on forest floors across East Asia.

Needlelike leaves grow in bundles, called fascicles.

Armand pine

(Pinus armandii)

This is one of many species of conifers that grow in the cool East Asian forests, especially at high altitudes. Its large, nutlike seeds are a favorite food of birds such as nutcrackers. These birds, which are members of the crow family, help to disperse the pine seeds.

Stone oak

(Lithocarpus sp.)

Evergreen stone oaks are especially diverse in tropical Southeast Asia and reach their northernmost limit in the Qinling. Their tough, leathery leaves are retained through the winter, and hard, stonelike acorns are produced in summer and fall.

Chinese chestnut

(Castanea mollissima)

This deciduous species is one of the most common chestnuts in East Asia. It has been planted for its ornamental leaves and nutritious nuts for so long that no one knows where it first grew in the wild.

Its leaves turn yellow in fall.

Chinese elm

(Ulmus parvifolia)

One of the hardiest elm species, the Chinese elm survives in freezing Siberia as well as the tropics—especially in the cooler mountain regions. In the mild climate of the Qinling, this elm is semi-deciduous, meaning it drops its leaves for a short time, just during the coldest weeks.

Chestnuts are produced in a spiny casing.

Woody grass

Bamboos are the tallest members of the grass family. The woody stems support their great height. Unlike the tapering trunks of most trees, bamboo stems keep the same thickness all the way to the top.

Bamboo

Nearly 1,500 species of bamboo can be found in tropical and temperate regions worldwide, with hundreds in China alone. They grow fast, reaching heights of about 35 in (90 cm) in a day. Thick, underground stems, called rhizomes, help bamboo spread quickly. This makes them form tall, dense clumps, providing shelter and food for many animals.

Hollow stems

The wood of trees is made of layers of tiny transport pipes packed into the trunk's core. But bamboo and other grasses have a hollow core instead of solid wood. Inside the stem, hard fibers grow between scattered bundles of transport pipes. This helps to strengthen their tubelike stems.

Flowers

Bamboos have more protein than many other kinds of vegetation. This helps nourish bamboo-eating animals like pandas. However, the plants die after flowering, and when many of them flower at once, the resulting loss of crop can mean starvation for pandas across their range.

Flowers spread their pollen in the wind.

Bamboo eaters

Although a member of the carnivorous bear family, the giant panda is adapted to feed almost entirely on bamboo. Its paws have a special raised wrist bone that works like a thumb to help grasp bamboo shoots.

Sooty bushtit

(Aegithalos fuliginosus)

Sooty bushtit is the eastern cousin of the European long-tailed tit. It is found only in the mountains of central China, where it flits through the shrub layer of the bamboo forest in groups of up to 40.

It has a long, narrow tail.

Squeaking silk moth

(Rhodinia fugax)

This insect is found throughout the mountains of temperate East Asia. The squeaking silk moth gets its name from the caterpillar's ability to squeak by forcing air through its breathing holes. The caterpillar spins a silk cocoon to change into a flying adult.

The caterpillars are green and can camouflage among vegetation.

Caterpillar

Animals of the Qinling deciduous forests

In the bamboo forests of the Qinling, the wildlife includes Asian species that have come from the cold northern regions and the tropics further south. With sunny summers and cool winters, this rich habitat is home to furry monkeys, colorful pheasants, and vegetarian bears. It also shelters giant amphibians that inhabit chilly mountain streams.

Qinling panda

(Ailuropoda melanoleuca qinlingensis)

These rare pandas live high in the Qinling and are named after the mountains they call home. Unlike their black-and-white cousins, they have a coat of brown and white. The special coloring helps them blend into their forest surroundings. This makes it easier for them to stay hidden among the trees, rocks, and plants in their habitat.

Chinese mountain snake

(Plagiopholis styani)

A reptile that survives in the cool mountains, this is a nonvenomous snake. Active at night, it burrows through the soil and litter of the mountain forest to catch earthworms and other invertebrate prey.

Golden snub-nosed monkey

(Rhinopithecus roxellana)

A thick coat of fur helps the golden snub-nosed monkey stay warm in these frosty forests. It is found only in the mountains of central China and mainly eats lichens that grow on trees.

Chinese giant salamander

(Andrias davidianus)

The world's biggest living amphibian, the Chinese giant salamander is found only in the Qinling, where it lurks in cold, fast-flowing streams. This secretive creature can grow to weigh as much as an average young teenage child. It breathes by absorbing oxygen from the water through its loose, folded skin.

Golden pheasant

(Chrysolophus pictus)

East Asia's mountain forests have a remarkable diversity of colorful pheasants. Only males have striking plumage and long tails, which they use to attract mates. While golden pheasants are native to China, they have also been introduced to other parts of the world.

Red panda

This red panda knows how to relax—draped lazily along a tree branch as if it were made just for napping. Found in China and the Himalayas, red pandas are much smaller than the giant panda, and spend much of their time climbing trees. They eat bamboo and can grasp stems with their front paws. Despite their name, red pandas are not members of the bear family—and are more closely related to raccoons, weasels, and otters.

FACT FILE

Area
238,870 miles² (618,670 km²)

Average rainfall
24 in (600 mm) annually

Average temperature
82°F (28°C) to 14°F (–10°C)

South Australian eucalyptus forests

Australia has especially distinctive forests—with lofty eucalyptus trees, curious marsupial mammals, and stretches of sandy red land.

Around three-quarters of the forests in Australia are dominated by eucalyptus trees, which have the greatest diversity on this island continent. Some species thrive in the wet eastern forests, while others are found in dry southern woodlands. The drier forests have a temperate climate with hot, parched summers, and many plant and animal species are found only here.

Hollows in eucalyptus trunks are often home to small animals such as the common brushtail possum.

Eucalyptus trees

There are more than 700 species of eucalyptus, from giants that rank among the tallest on the planet to short sprawling shrubs. Eucalyptus leaves are thick and oily, making them tough to digest. However, some animals have evolved to eat them and little else.

Bushfires

Wildfires that burn through the scrubland vegetation of Australia are called bushfires. They often begin naturally, due to lightning strikes igniting dry plants. As the forest catches fire, the flames also burn through the leaf litter, enriching the soil with ash. Bushfires clear the forest canopy and allow more sunlight to reach the ground, so new shoots can grow.

Geography of the south Australian eucalyptus forests

At the southern end of the world, Australia's forests border an island continent dominated by a vast central desert. Trees grow in rain-fed coastal climates, but to the south, summers stay hot and dry, with wildfires being a common threat. A special kind of forest thrives here—a land of hundreds of eucalyptus species, home to many plants and animals found nowhere else on Earth.

Gondawanan origins

Long ago, Australia was joined with Antarctica, South America, Africa, India, and New Zealand as part of a great southern supercontinent called Gondwana. Many plants and animals, such as Australian eucalyptus trees, southern beeches, and pouched marsupials, first evolved here and still remain confined to the southern hemisphere.

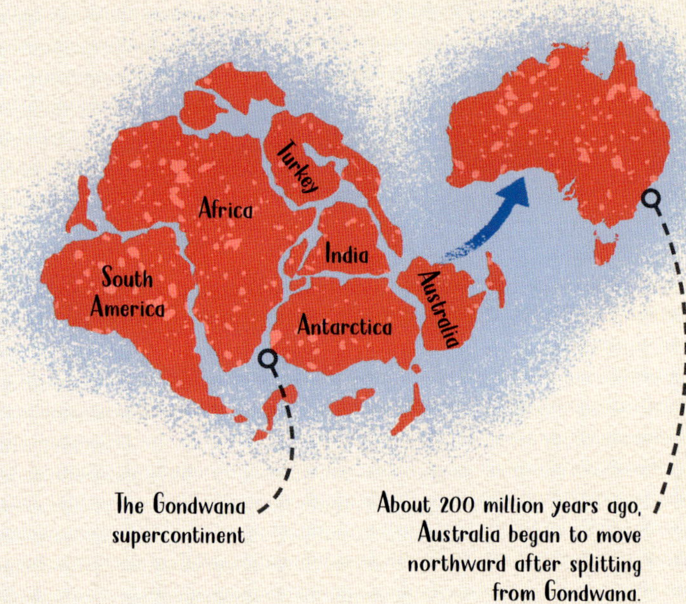

The Gondwana supercontinent

About 200 million years ago, Australia began to move northward after splitting from Gondwana.

Mediterranean-type climate

Several places around the world experience a Mediterranean-type climate—with cool, wet winters and hot, dry summers. These include California, Chile, South Africa, southern Australia, and the Mediterranean basin itself. Many plants and animals here are adapted to cope with seasonal challenges, such as droughts and wildfires.

This type of climate is usually seen on western and southern sides of continents.

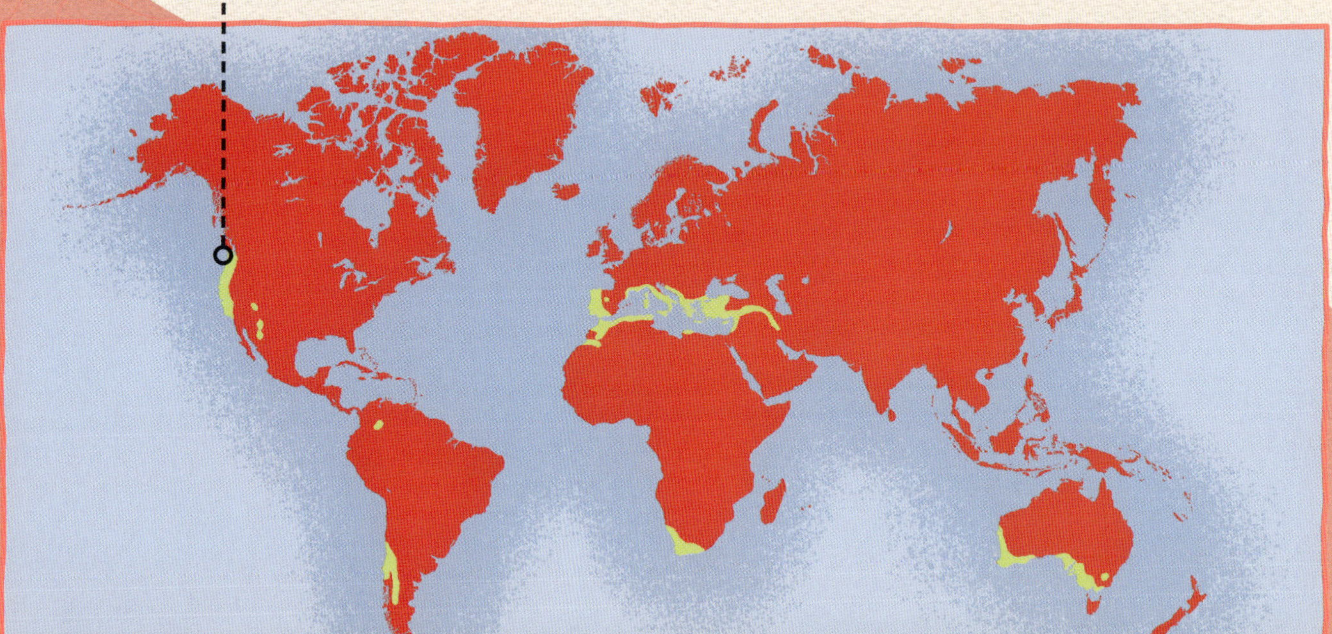

Moist highland habitats

In the eastern parts of southern Australia, the Flinders, Lofty, and Olary ranges block the summer rain from reaching the far side. As a result, the Mediterranean-type forests here are wetter than those along the lowland coasts. Eucalyptus trees share this damp habitat with other moisture-loving plants, such as oaks, wattles, and pines.

Southwest hot spot

For more than 200 million years, the southwest corner of Australia has had a stable ice-free climate, making it one of the world's oldest habitats. Thousands of species such as the Albany pitcher plant changed and adapted over millions of years, with almost no contact from the outside world.

Mallee

On the poorest sandy soils of southern Australia, forests are replaced by mallee—a type of open woodland with small trees and scattered woody shrubs. In places such as the Eyre Peninsula, these woodlands thin out even more, giving way to open heathland and dunes.

Coral vine
(Kennedia coccinea)

This evergreen vine is found only on the sandy soils of southwest Australia. It is named after its vibrant, coral-colored flowers. Coral vine is a legume—a member of the bean, pea, and clover family—with heart-shaped leaves and seeds that grow in beanlike pods.

Western black tea tree
(Melaleuca lanceolata)

Like other tea trees, the western black tea tree is a relative of eucalyptus found in drier parts of Australia. Its branches are tipped with fuzzy brushlike flower spikes. The tree's papery bark burns quickly in passing wildfires, helping it survive in the fire-prone region.

Plants of the south Australian eucalyptus forests

Plants that grow in Mediterranean climates often have small, leathery leaves that can hold water during the hot, dry summers. Most are evergreen and keep their leaves all year. However, a few species are summer-deciduous, which means they shed their leaves in the dry season instead of winter. Many of Australia's plants belong to groups that are largely confined to the southern hemisphere.

Jarrah
(Eucalyptus marginata)

Eucalyptus trees that grow in the wettest soils can reach impressive heights. Jarrah, with its stringy, fibrous bark, is one of the tallest species in Australia. It grows well in moist river valleys and on mountain ranges. Jarrah forests support a large diversity of plant and animal life.

Sandhill wattle

(Acacia ligulata)

Wattles are cousins of the flat-topped acacias that dot Africa's savannas. The sandhill wattle shares the family's distinctive features—divided leaves, seed pods, and its place among the legumes. It is widespread across the sandy soils of Australia's arid interior—hence its name.

Mallee

(Eucalyptus diversifolia)

This eucalyptus species has smooth bark and it gives its name to the Mallee plant community. Mallee often grows as a low-branching shrub. Its flowers have large, fluffy stalks, called stamens, at the center, which produce pollen. These flowers attract a wide variety of insects and birds that visit them for nectar.

Grey saltbush

(Atriplex cinerea)

Salt tolerance helps the grey saltbush grow in coastal regions near the sea and around salt lakes farther inland. It survives by storing excess salt in special glands in its leaves. This hardy shrub spreads across nutrient-poor soils and shifting dunes, making it one of the few species that can grow there.

Its creamy white flowers grow in clusters of nine or more.

Each flower spike is a cluster of hundreds of tiny individual blooms.

Swamp banksia

(Banksia littoralis)

Named after its wet riverside habitat, swamp banksia grows along the south Australian coastline. This plant has rough, crumbly bark and produces large nectar-rich flower spikes. The blossoms are especially known for their warm scent of baked bread.

Surviving fire

The scorching summers of Mediterranean-type climate can ignite parched vegetation, with seasonal winds fanning the flames. Wildfires race through forests and shrubland, destroying foliage and turning wood to cinder. But many trees and plants that grow in southern Australia are adapted to survive these harsh conditions.

Flammable trees

The leaves of eucalyptus and related trees are packed with bitter oils that deter plant eaters. The same oils also make the trees highly flammable, causing them to burn quickly as fire sweeps across the land. However, these trees are remarkably resilient and can regenerate after a blaze.

Surviving as seeds

While parent plants may perish in fires, their seeds ensure the next generation lives on. Some Australian plants such as banksias store seeds in fire-resistant cones. These cones open only after a fire, scattering the seeds on the ground. Others like wattles release their seeds before the fire, allowing them to get buried and survive underground. After the fire, these seeds sprout in ash-rich soil.

Regenerating after fire

Thick bark helps protect some trees from fire. But if the trunk burns, many eucalyptus trees can regrow from a swollen base at the tree's foot. This structure is shielded from the flames, allowing living tissue inside to produce new shoots and bring the tree back to life.

Animals of the south Australian eucalyptus forests

Animals that live in these eucalyptus forests must cope with dry, scorching summers and other extreme conditions. Many have special adaptations—some can digest tough, oily leaves of eucalyptus and similar trees, while others have evolved unique body parts to find food in hard-to-reach places. A few are predators that use speed or sharp senses to hunt. All face long droughts and occasional outbreaks of fire.

Numbat

(Myrmecobius fasciatus)

Many of Australia's mammals eat ants and termites, which are a reliable source of food even during the dry season. The numbat is one such marsupial found only in southwest Australia. Like an anteater, it uses its long tongue to lap up thousands of termites each day.

It sports a striking white band on its tail.

Baudin's black cockatoo

(Zanda baudinii)

Cockatoos make up a family of parrots native to Australia. Unlike their brightly colored tropical cousins, most cockatoos are black or white. One of them is the Baudin's black cockatoo, which is confined only to southwest Australia.

Short-beaked echidna

(Tachyglossus aculeatus)

The short-beaked echidna is a monotreme—an egg-laying mammal—and a close relative of the platypus. Also known as Australia's spiny anteater, it probes the ground with its short, sensitive beak. Then it flicks out a long tongue to slurp up ants and termites.

Redback spider

(Latrodectus hasselti)

The redback spider spins its web close to the ground, stretching it between two flat surfaces to trap crawling insects and other invertebrates. This spider is also found in urban spaces, and its highly toxic venom is dangerous for humans, too. So it's best to observe this spider from a safe distance.

Mallee fowl

(Leipoa ocellata)

This ground-dwelling bird lays its eggs in large mounds of rotting vegetation. The heat from the decaying material keeps the eggs warm until they hatch. As soon as mallee fowl chicks emerge, they dig their way out and begin fending for themselves.

Common brushtail possum

(Trichosurus vulpecula)

This climbing marsupial is found in forests across Australia but is most at home in the dry eucalyptus woodlands of the south. Like koalas that lounge in Australia's wetter eastern forests, the brushtail possum eats eucalyptus leaves and can digest their tough fiber and pungent oils.

This python gets its name from the woven carpetlike pattern on its skin.

Carpet python

(Morelia spilota)

Australia's hot, dry habitats are ideal for sunbathing reptiles, so the continent hosts many lizards and snakes. The carpet python is one of the most widespread. Like other pythons, it isn't venomous. Instead, it wraps itself around its prey and squeezes it still before feeding. This python's meals include many birds and mammals.

Quokka

Australia is a land where most native mammals are marsupials—animals that start life in their mother's pouch. The quokka is one of them, a rabbit-sized member of the wallaby-kangaroo family. After leaving the pouch, baby quokkas, or joeys, stay with their moms for more than a year. Like many marsupial species, they have a restricted habitat and are found only in the forests and shrubland of southwest Australia.

Tropical forests

With year-round warmth and heavy rain, life thrives in tropical rainforests. These regions support more kinds of plants, fungi, insects, and birds than anywhere else in the world. In some places, rain falls throughout the year and these forests have a steady supply of flowers and fruit. In the tropical dry forests, rain is seasonal and life must cope with long, dry seasons when many trees lose their leaves.

FACT FILE

Area
95,251 miles^2
(246,700 km^2)

Average rainfall
98 in (2,500 mm) annually

Average temperature
84°F (29°C)

Central Amazonian várzea rainforests

Deep within the Amazon rainforest, the mighty river rises and transforms the land into a vast, seasonally flooded rainforest known as várzea.

So much rain falls over the Amazon basin that, during the wettest months, the rivers overflow and flood the forests, sending water high up the tree trunks. Terrestrial and aquatic life come together, with birds and monkeys feeding in treetops and fishes swimming in the dark waters below.

Living between two worlds

Ground-living animals face some of the biggest challenges here. As the water levels rise, some move off to higher, drier regions. Others stay and spend more of their time swimming from place to place.

Tapirs, the largest mammals in the Amazon basin, are excellent swimmers.

Flooded forests

Plants in the várzea have special adaptations to grow well in the ever-changing conditions. Trees are tall enough to hold their foliage above the rising water and have roots that can withstand flooding. Other plants survive as epiphytes and climbers, clinging to the branches of other trees.

Amazon basin

The forests of northern South America are shaped by Solimões—the section of the upper Amazon River in northwestern Brazil and its many tributaries. Together, they form the world's biggest river systems—the Amazon basin. Rain and melting snow from the Andes Mountains flow into these rivers, which carry the water on a winding journey east, all the way to the Atlantic Ocean.

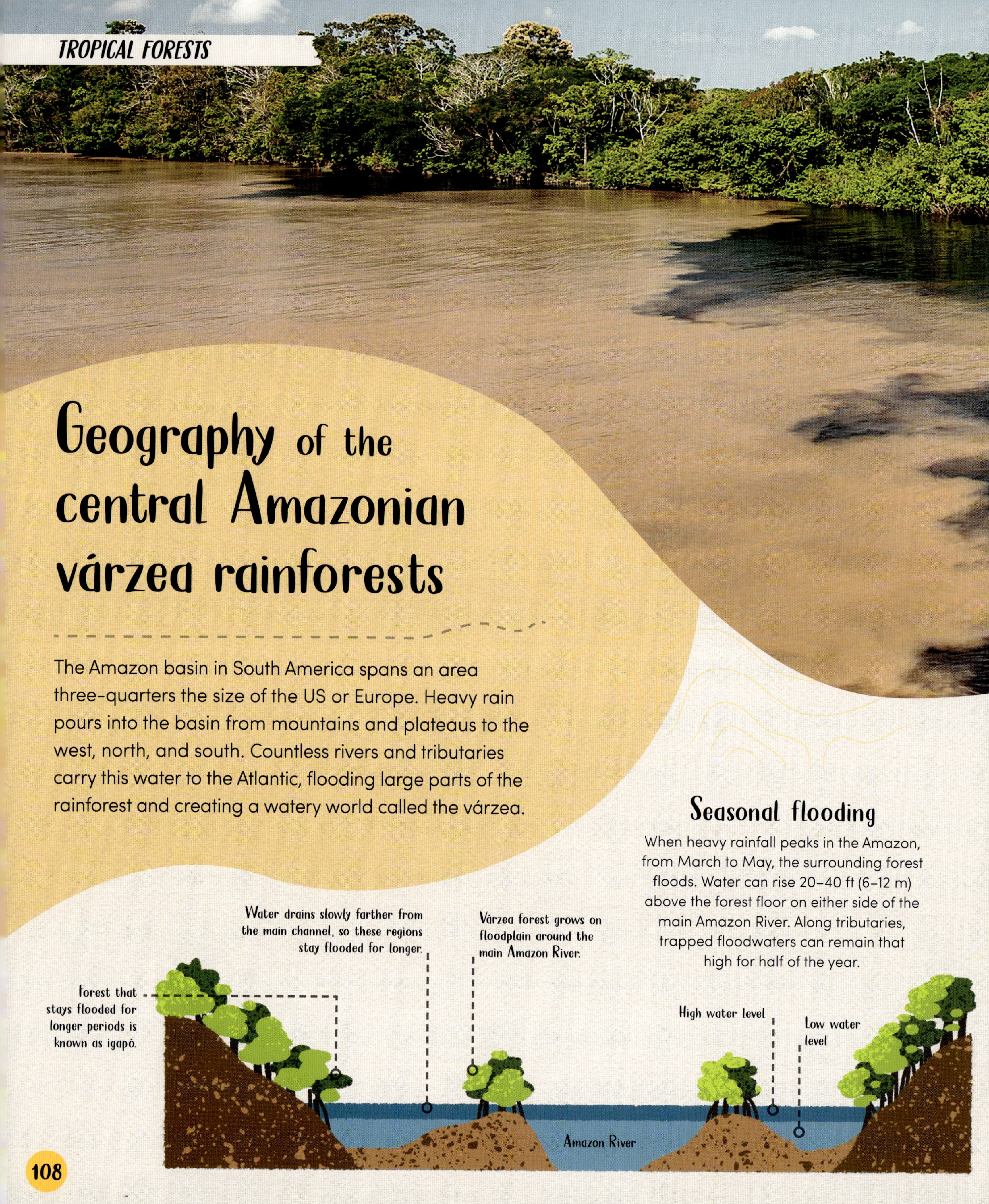

Geography of the central Amazonian várzea rainforests

The Amazon basin in South America spans an area three-quarters the size of the US or Europe. Heavy rain pours into the basin from mountains and plateaus to the west, north, and south. Countless rivers and tributaries carry this water to the Atlantic, flooding large parts of the rainforest and creating a watery world called the várzea.

Seasonal flooding

When heavy rainfall peaks in the Amazon, from March to May, the surrounding forest floods. Water can rise 20–40 ft (6–12 m) above the forest floor on either side of the main Amazon River. Along tributaries, trapped floodwaters can remain that high for half of the year.

Whitewater and blackwater

Vast amounts of sediment are swept down from the Andes Mountains to the west. In the upper Amazon, known as Solimões, this sediment turns the water a cloudy pale brown. These stretches are called "whitewater." In tributaries such as the Rio Negro, the water is much clearer but stained dark brown by dead leaves, earning it the name "blackwater."

Where river and tributaries join, whitewaters and blackwaters flow side by side before mixing together.

Vegetation in the várzea

Trees that grow in the várzea tolerate flooding around their trunks, while their foliage remains above water. Unlike other rainforests, few shrubs and ground-level plants grow here, as many cannot survive being fully submerged so long.

Some trees have arching "stilt" roots that make them more stable on flooded ground.

Nutrient recycling

Everything is quickly recycled in the Amazon basin. Water vapor rises as steam from the warm, wet forests, condenses into thick clouds, then falls again as rain. Minerals washed down from the mountains and released from dead leaves nourish plants and enter food chains in both river and forest.

Plants of the central Amazonian várzea rainforests

The Amazon basin has more plant species than anywhere else in the world. They grow wherever the sunlight can sneak in—from the shadowy forest floor to the mossy branches high in the canopy. Many plants are epiphytes, which grow perched on branches. Climbing vines also thrive here, twisting through the forest and making up much of the rainforest's plant diversity

Water hyacinth

(Eichhornia crassipes)

Water hyacinths form thick mats on the surface of rivers and lakes, with their roots dangling beneath the water. As they drift across open water, they absorb more sunlight, far from the shade of the tree canopy.

Foliage of an "emergent" kapok tree towers over the rest of the rainforest canopy.

Philodendron

(Philodendron sp.)

Climbing philodendrons start life as tiny seeds that germinate on the forest floor. Using tree trunks for support, they climb upward to reach the sunlight above the dense canopy. Once they reach the light, they begin to flower and grow bigger leaves.

The climber clings to the trunk with grasping roots.

Amazon water lily

(Victoria amazonica)

Giant water lilies in the Amazon can grow some of the world's biggest leaves—up to 10 ft (3 m) wide. Rooted in the river bottom, their stalks reach the surface, where floating leaves spread large enough to support the weight of a small child.

Each leaf is strengthened by a network of stiff ribs and veins.

Flaming sword bromeliad

(Vriesea sp.)

Bromeliads belong to the pineapple family and are mostly found in the American tropics. Most species such as the flaming sword grow as epiphytes in the canopy without harming the tree.

Small animals, like insects and tree frogs, often live in the pools of rainwater that collect in the cupped leaves.

Kapok

(Ceiba pentandra)

The kapok is one of the tallest trees in the Amazon basin, reaching more than 200 ft (60 m) high. The base of its trunk is supported by wide, wall-like structures called buttresses. These help the tree stay upright on wet, unstable ground and survive heavy flooding.

Clusters of hanging fruit attract fruit eaters, such as macaws, toucans, and monkeys.

Moriche palm

(Mauritia flexuosa)

Hundreds of palm species are found in the Amazon rainforest, many adapted to the low light beneath the canopy. But the moriche palm is a giant of the swampy várzea. It drops fruit that are carried by floodwaters to new places to grow.

Animals of the central Amazonian várzea rainforests

From the rich canopy to the forest floor, and from seasonal floods to solid ground, the várzea forest is teeming with different habitats. Monkeys climb and swing through the treetops, while fish and reptiles glide through the waters below. Some animals live here year-round, while others visit only when the forest is dry or deeply flooded.

Bald uakari monkey

(Cacajao calvus)

The bald uakari monkey spends all its time in the várzea. When the forest is flooded, it is confined to the canopy—feeding on shoots, fruit, and small animals. When the waters recede, it climbs down to the forest floor to search for fallen seeds.

Green anaconda

(Eunectes murinus)

The world's heaviest snake mostly lives in water and can hold its breath for about 10 minutes. The green anaconda is a constrictor, which means it kills prey by wrapping its coils tightly around the animal until the prey's heart stops beating. It dines on animals as large as adult caimans.

The vivid pattern on its skin warns predators that it is poisonous.

Brilliant-thighed poison frog

(Allobates femoralis)

Like many frogs in the wet rainforest, this species lays eggs on solid ground. When they hatch, the father carries the tadpoles on his back, and releases them into pools as the floodwaters rise.

Black caiman

(Melanosuchus niger)

South America's biggest reptile, the black caiman is a top predator in the Amazon. In the drier season, the female lays eggs in a nest of leaf litter on the forest floor. The mother guards the nest until the babies hatch, ready to swim in the floodwaters. When threatened, the babies call out to their mother for help.

Pink-toe tarantula

(Avicularia avicularia)

Hundreds of tarantula species live in rainforests. Some live on the ground, while others such as this pink-toe tarantula inhabit trees—safely above the floodwaters. Although popularly called "bird eaters," these spiders mostly prey on insects.

Hoatzin

(Opisthocomus hoazin)

The Amazon basin's strangest bird is the hoatzin, which feeds mainly on leaves—unusual for birds. Its flightless chicks are born with claws on their wings. This unique adaptation allows them to climb out of treetop nests and avoid falling into the floodwaters below.

Lowland tapir

(Tapirus terrestris)

The lowland tapir is South America's largest mammal and a long-nosed relative of horses and rhinoceroses. It is at home both on land and in water. Young tapirs have striped fur to help camouflage them from predators in the sun-dappled forest.

A tapir uses its long nose as a snorkel while swimming.

Each wing has two claws that are used to grip branches.

Arapaima

(Arapaima gigas)

Arapaima is among the world's largest freshwater fishes. It can breathe air even when the oxygen levels drop in water. As the floodwaters rise, the female lays eggs in an underwater nest. The male protects the newly hatched fry by keeping them in his mouth.

Freshwater fish

The Amazon basin is where some of the world's richest forests meet its greatest diversity of freshwater fish. Three-quarters of the fish species here belong to just three groups: characins, cichlids, and catfish. They swim between the trees of the flooded várzea forest, taking advantage of the seasonal rise in waters to lay eggs and feed.

Freshwater fish hot spot

Half of all the world's fish species live in freshwater, and more glide through the waters of the Amazon basin than anywhere else. More than 3,000 species are known from the region, many restricted to certain tributaries, with more discovered each year.

This large piranha species mainly preys on other fish.

Red-bellied piranha

Aimara wolf fish

Characins

Characins include hundreds of species—from tiny, brightly colored tetras to large predators like piranhas. Most are midwater fish that often swim in shoals and have sharp, gripping teeth to snap up prey.

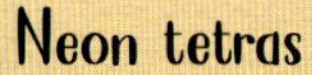

Neon tetras

Pike characin

Cichlids

While most fish scatter their eggs and abandon their young, cichlids stand out for their parenting. These fish lay eggs on rocks or leaves and guard them from predators. Some species—called mouthbrooders—even scoop up babies into their mouths to keep them safe.

Catfish

With mouths tucked under their head, most catfish grub around on the riverbed for food. Some, such as panaques, even munch on wood from fallen branches—scraping off soft, nutritious algae. A few may even be able to digest the wood they chew.

Sweet treat

Overhanging tree branches drop fruit and seeds into water, providing a tasty treat for some Amazon fish. A few, such as the piraputanga, a type of large characin, leap out of the water to pluck a meal straight from the tree.

Giant otter

The Amazon basin is home to the world's largest otter species—the giant otter. This animal is an expert fisher and takes advantage of the river system's enormous bounty of fish, including catfish and piranhas. The thick defensive scales of this armored catfish are no match for the sharp teeth and powerful jaws of this river predator.

FACT FILE

Area
11,965 miles² (30,990 km²)

Average rainfall
133 in (3,380 mm) annually

Average temperature
79°F (26°C)

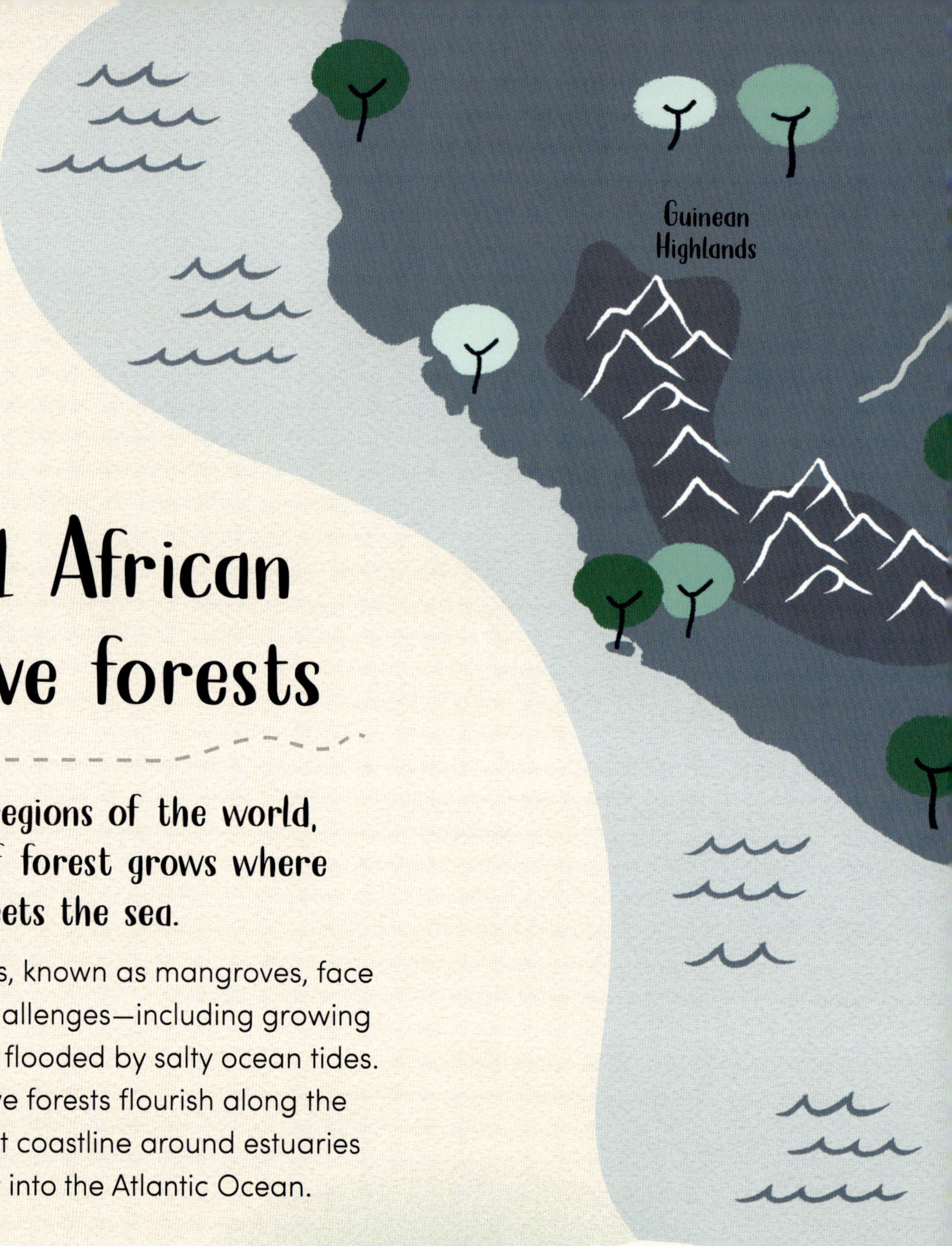

Guinean Highlands

Central African mangrove forests

In the tropical regions of the world, a distinct type of forest grows where land meets the sea.

The trees in these forests, known as mangroves, face some of the toughest challenges—including growing on soft ground regularly flooded by salty ocean tides. In Africa, the mangrove forests flourish along the continent's central-west coastline around estuaries of rivers that empty into the Atlantic Ocean.

Fish out of water

Mangroves bring together animals from both land and sea. These include mudskippers, a type of fish that can walk over the mud during low tide. They live beneath mangrove branches, which also shelter insects, birds, and monkeys.

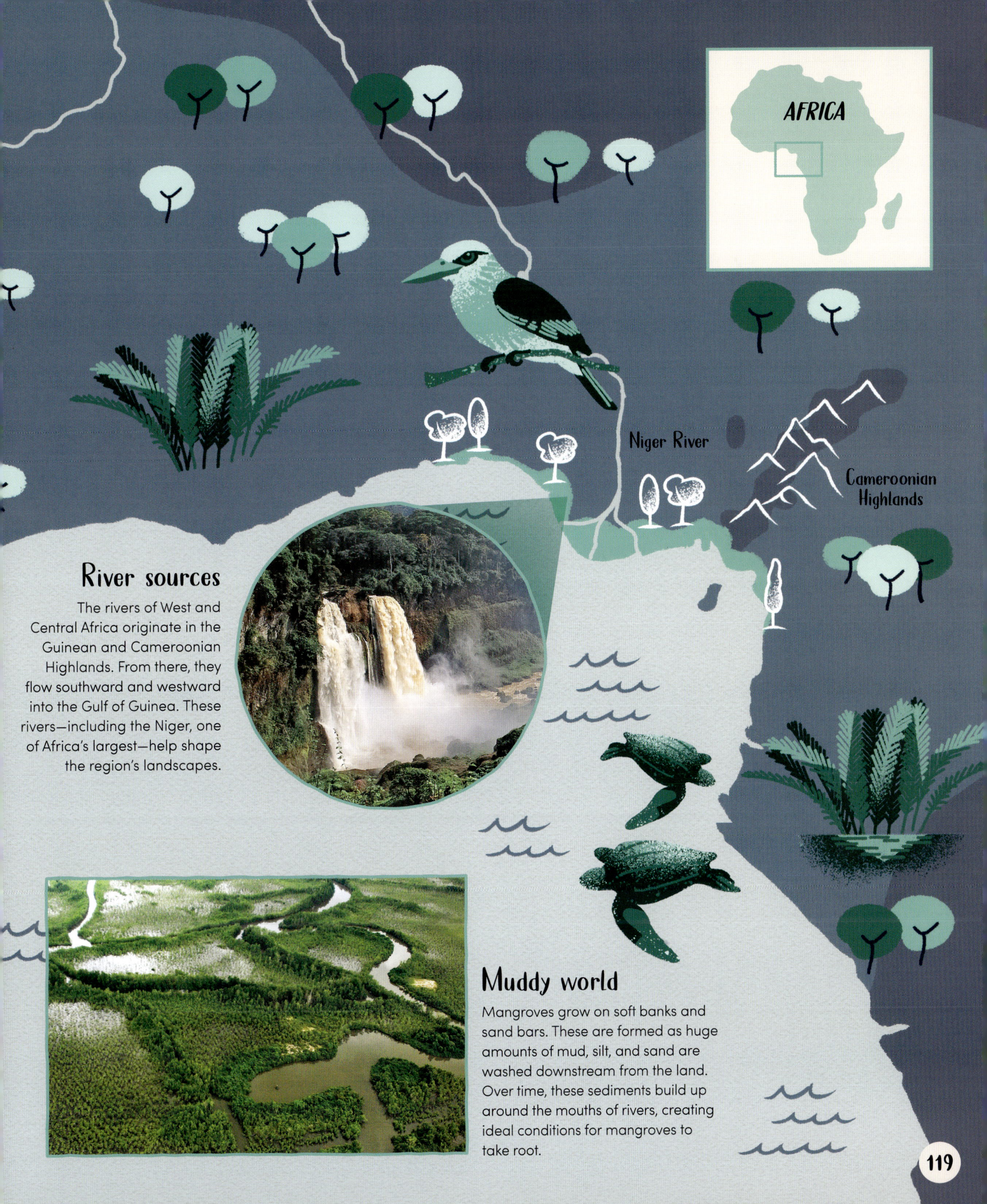

River sources

The rivers of West and Central Africa originate in the Guinean and Cameroonian Highlands. From there, they flow southward and westward into the Gulf of Guinea. These rivers—including the Niger, one of Africa's largest—help shape the region's landscapes.

Muddy world

Mangroves grow on soft banks and sand bars. These are formed as huge amounts of mud, silt, and sand are washed downstream from the land. Over time, these sediments build up around the mouths of rivers, creating ideal conditions for mangroves to take root.

Coastal muds

Mangroves grow best where the mud is thickest. This helps their roots go deeper into the ground, provides stability, and keeps them from falling over on the soft, shifting coastline. The mangrove trees can even survive in areas flooded by salty seawater.

Geography of the central African mangrove forests

In central-west Africa—along the coastlines of Nigeria, Cameroon, and Gabon—mangrove forests are shaped by the rivers and the sea. Freshwater from rivers pours into estuaries, making the seawater less salty around the mudflats, where many mangroves thrive. But they also grow on saltier mud where ocean tides form offshore lagoons, especially in the far-west region.

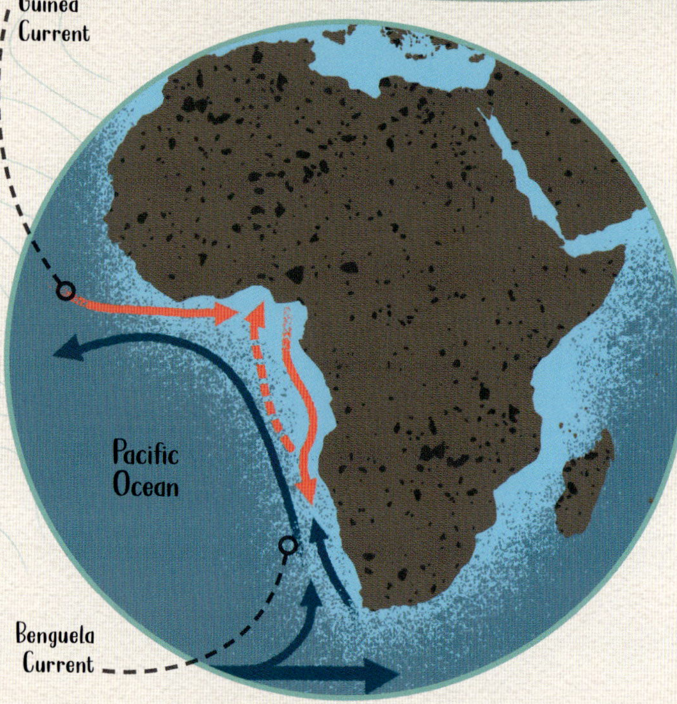

Marine currents

The central-west African coastline is affected by two oceanic currents—the warmer Guinea Current from the north and the cooler Benguela Current from the south. These currents carry nutrients and sediments that help mangrove forests flourish and stay rich.

Mangrove forest at low tide

Mangrove forest at high tide

Tidal influence

Like most ocean shorelines around the world, central-west Africa experiences a daily cycle of two high tides and two low tides. During low tide, mudflats are exposed. At high tide, the area is flooded and the bases of the trees are submerged so that only their leaves remain above water, exposed to air.

Monthly and seasonal changes

Twice a month, the tidal flow reaches its maximum. During this time, tides rise to their highest, and many fish spawn among the mangrove roots. The annual wet season brings even more water flooding down from the rivers.

The highest water levels are called spring tides.

White mangrove

(Laguncularia racemosa)

The white mangrove belongs to a family of tropical bushwillow trees. It grows around bays on higher ground, further inland than other mangrove trees. As a result, high ocean tides rarely reach it.

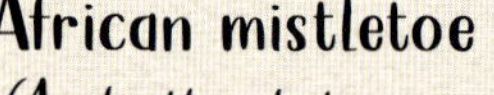

African mistletoe

(Agelanthus heteromorphus)

Like other mistletoe species, this plant is a parasite. It grows on the branches of trees found in the inland swamp forests. Its special roots tap into the branches to extract water and minerals from the tree's transport pipes.

Thanks to the mistletoe's green leaves, it can make its own sugar by photosynthesis.

Plants of the central African mangrove forests

Few plant species can survive the challenges of living between the tides. Conditions here are much harder than in the freshwater swamp forests and rainforests found farther inland. This is because only some plants, called halophytes, have special ways to adapt to the saltiness of seawater. Among these halophytes are several species of mangrove trees that flourish in large numbers along the African coastline.

Halophytes

Some halophytes such as the leathery-leaved mangrove fern grow only in the tropics, just like mangrove trees. But others, such as saltwort and sea grapes, can be found throughout the world. They thrive on bare mud before mangrove forests replace them.

Mangrove fern

Sea grapes

Saltwort

Red mangrove

(Rhizophora mangle)

The red mangrove gets extra support on the soft mud by growing "stilt" roots that arch down from the tree's trunk. These roots spread the tree's weight over a wide area and can also take in extra oxygen directly from the air.

Nipa palm

(Nypa fruticans)

This salt-tolerant swamp palm was once found only in the Indo-Pacific but has now taken over tropical coastlines around the world. In some places, it covers the mud in huge numbers, even stopping native mangroves from thriving.

Large, divided leaves grow up from an underground stem beneath the water.

Black mangrove

(Avicennia germinans)

Upward-pointing roots that breathe air help this mangrove survive in thick, oxygen-poor mud. These roots, called pneumatophores, form a spiky carpet around the base of the tree's trunk.

Mangrove trees

Different kinds of mangrove trees may look alike, but they belong to unrelated plant families. Each has evolved similar adaptations to survive in salty, flooded habitats. Besides tolerating seawater, they grow in oxygen-poor mud.

Salt tolerance

Mangroves cope with salt in different ways. Black mangroves, which grow in the saltiest mud, release excess salt through special glands in their leaves. Red mangroves use their roots to filter out salt from the seawater before it travels up into their foliage.

Red mangrove leaves are shiny and dark green on top, with a lighter, yellow-green underside.

Roots

Plants need oxygen from the air, just like us—but roots buried in wet mud can't breathe easily. Different mangroves have different types of roots to absorb oxygen from the air above the mudflat—especially at low tide.

Stilt roots

Downward-curving roots of the red mangrove stay exposed to air even in the deep water at high tide, letting the plant breathe.

The roots have "breathing" pores that enable them to absorb oxygen from air.

Snorkel roots

Upward-pointing roots of the black mangrove, called pneumatophores, reach the air only in shallow water at low tide.

Knee roots

Arching roots of the white mangrove take in air from farther inland, where the ground is usually flooded by the tide.

A short stalk keeps the germinating seed attached to the parent tree.

Setting seed

Mangrove seeds can float and survive in salty water. In some species, like the red mangrove, seeds begin to germinate while still attached to the tree. This helps their long shoots to anchor firmly in the mud when they eventually fall.

The long beanlike growth is called a propagule.

Mangrove zonation

Some mangroves grow better in deeper water than others. So the forest gradually changes from sea to land. Red mangroves grow closest to the shore followed by black mangroves, and finally white mangroves farther inland.

Sclater's guenon
(Cercopithecus sclateri)

Found only in southern Nigeria, this fruit-eating monkey lives in swampy forests and sometimes ventures into the coastal mangroves. Once more widespread, it is now endangered due to deforestation.

Dugong
(Dugong dugong)

This air-breathing sea mammal is a cousin of the freshwater manatee. It grazes on seagrasses growing in sheltered lagoons and channels lined with mangrove forests. The dugong gives birth in shallows along the coast.

Animals of the central African mangrove forests

The floor of the mangrove forest rarely dries out and is usually flooded with seawater. This means that most resident animals live in the higher branches or come from the sea. At high tide, fish swim among the roots. At low tide, mudskippers and crabs emerge to join visitors from forests farther inland.

Blue-breasted kingfisher

(Halcyon malimbica)

This bird watches for prey from a perch in the mangrove trees. Then, it swoops down to catch mudskippers or crabs at low tide. The blue-breasted kingfisher sometimes cracks open crab shells by smashing them on rocks.

Its skin releases an oily fluid that makes this hairless hippo look shiny.

Pygmy hippopotamus

(Choeropsis liberiensis)

Mostly active at night, this mammal lives in swamp forests upriver from the saltier mangroves. Like its larger relative, the pygmy hippopotamus spends a lot of time wallowing in water. It browses mainly on shrubs along well-worn land trails.

Like all marine turtles, the leatherback has flipperlike limbs for swimming.

Leatherback turtle

(Dermochelys coriacea)

The world's largest turtle, the leatherback spends most of its time swimming in the open ocean. It comes ashore only to lay and bury eggs. Some of its largest nesting sites are found along the mangrove-lined banks of West Africa.

Water chevrotain

(Hyemoschus aquaticus)

This small hoofed animal also lives in the swamp forests, where it dives underwater when threatened. It feeds mainly on fruit but visits the mangroves during low tide to catch the occasional crab or scavenge on dead fish.

West African mudskipper

(Periophthalmus barbarus)

Mudskippers are goby fish that can live on muddy seashores. They use their fins like legs to carry them out of water. To keep breathing, they rely on seawater stored in their gill chambers.

West African fiddler crab

When the tide is low, West African fiddler crabs emerge from burrows in the mud and scuttle beneath mangrove trees. Males have one huge claw, which they wave at other crabs to warn off rivals or impress a mate. With their smaller claw, they scoop up mud and pass it into their mouth, sifting algae and other tasty morsels.

FACT FILE

Area
16,792 miles² (43,490 km²)

Average rainfall
Dry season: 2.8 in (70 mm) per month
Wet season: 0.6 in (15 mm) per month

Average temperature
77°F (25°C)

Madagascan spiny forests

Sun-baked spiny giants and rare, leaping lemurs unite in this bizarre thorny world.

The island of Madagascar is known for its unique animals—including lemurs found nowhere else—but it is also a place of strikingly different forests. In the east, rainforests grow lush and green, while the west is dry, with a wooded landscape quite unlike any other.

With its spiny trunk and a crown of leaves, the bottle tree looks like a cross between a cactus and palm.

Ancient succulents

Plants in this forest may resemble desert cacti but are unrelated. They evolved in isolation, and their rich diversity comes from ancient origins. The spiny forest is Madagascar's oldest habitat and was once more widespread when the entire island was drier.

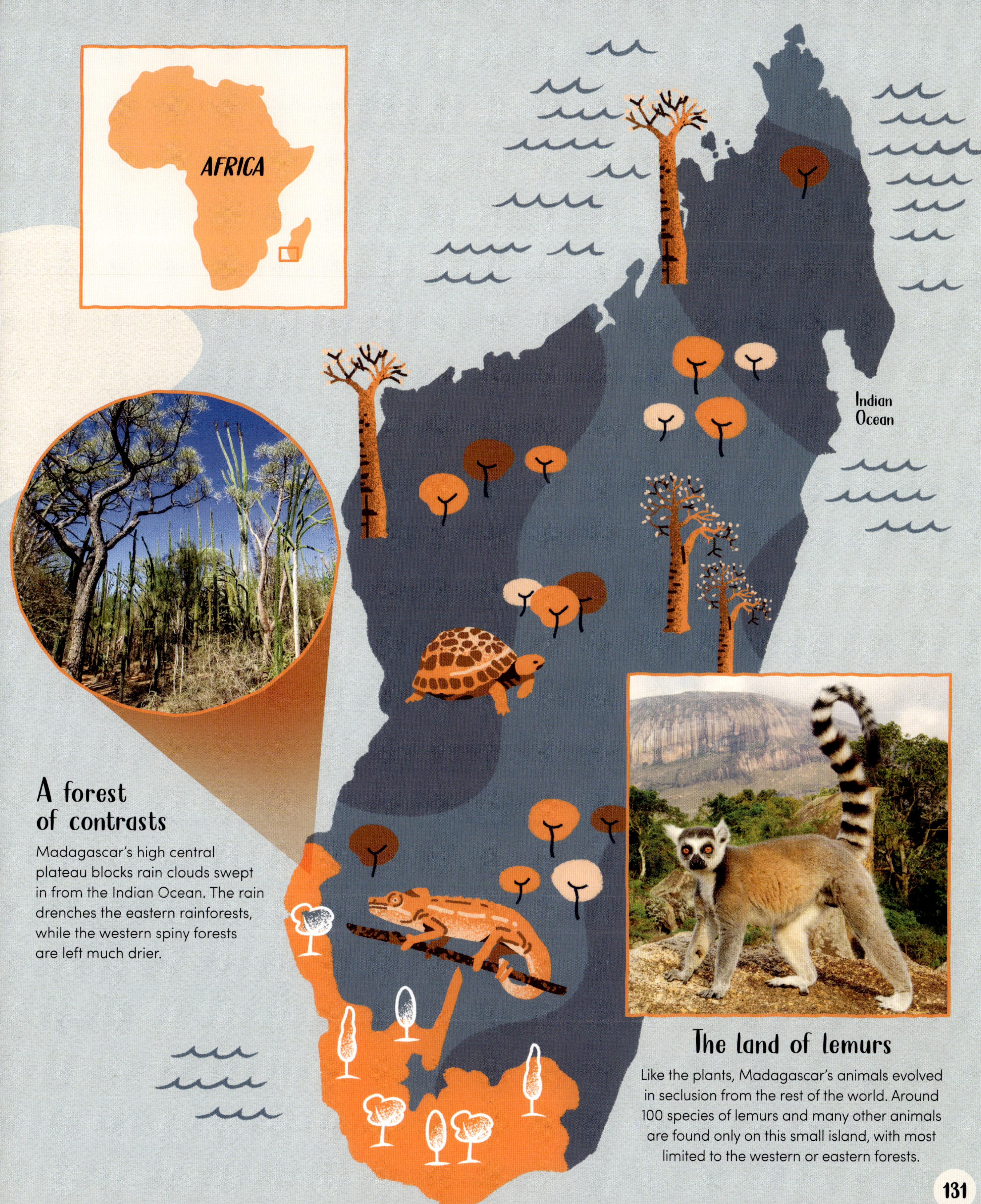

A forest of contrasts

Madagascar's high central plateau blocks rain clouds swept in from the Indian Ocean. The rain drenches the eastern rainforests, while the western spiny forests are left much drier.

The land of lemurs

Like the plants, Madagascar's animals evolved in seclusion from the rest of the world. Around 100 species of lemurs and many other animals are found only on this small island, with most limited to the western or eastern forests.

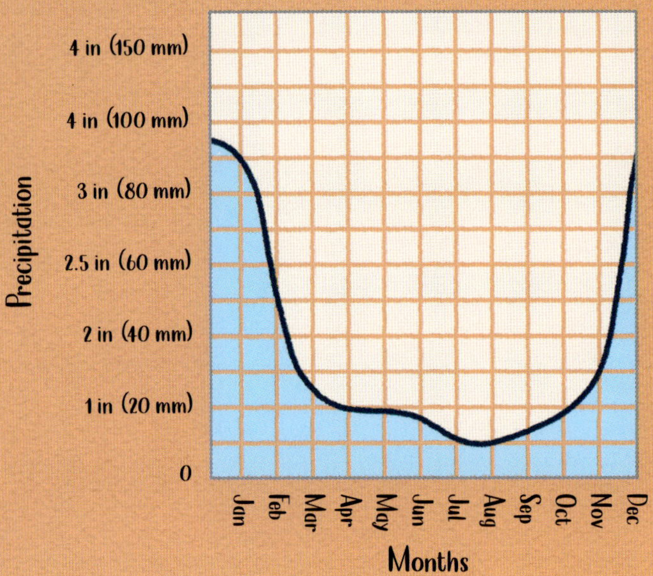

Seasonally dry tropics

A short period of heavy rains reaches southwest Madagascar from the Indian Ocean during the region's monsoon season. At other times, rainfall lacks the strength to cross the island's high central plateau, leaving the southwest as dry as a desert.

Rich habitat

Like many dry forests, Madagascar's spiny forests lack a closed canopy. This allows more sunlight to reach the ground, supporting a rich diversity of sprawling shrubs and other low-growing plants. However, it also means these forests do not have the layered structure typical of wetter rainforests.

Geography of the Madagascan spiny forests

Madagascar's west coast can get less than half of the yearly rainfall of Britain. Most of this falls within three months, leaving a long dry season for the rest of the year. The southwest region is the driest of all. This makes it an ideal home for the cactuslike plants of the Madagascan spiny forest.

The red "tsingy" is made from crumbly clay.

Rock types

Much of western Madagascar sits on chalky limestone rocks. They corrode under seasonal rainfall into a landscape of white, razor-sharp peaks, called tsingy. Similar peaks are also created when red clay is eroded following deforestation.

Retaining water

Trees and shrubs of seasonally dry tropical forests often share adaptations with desert plants. Many have thick leaves and water-storing stems, filled during the short rainy season.

Plants of the Madagascan spiny forests

Madagascar's spiny thickets contain more unique plant species than anywhere else on the island—over 90 percent grow only here. The forest is full of xerophytes—plants adapted to cope with long droughts during the harsh dry season. Many are succulents, with fleshy water-storing tissues.

Kalanchoe

(Kalanchoe beharensis)

The large fleshy leaves of kalanchoes swell with water during the rainy season and store it during drought. Tiny hairs on the leaves help reduce water loss from evaporation.

The bare branches give it the appearance of an upside-down tree.

Za baobab

(Adansonia za)

Although baobab trees are found across Africa and Australia, most species, such as the za baobab, are unique to Madagascar. Their thick, swollen trunks hold water to help them survive drought. During the dry season, they drop their leaves to reduce their need for water.

Succulent sesame

(Uncarina grandidieri)

The bright flowers of succulent sesame attract pollen-eating beetles. Instead of the usual dry grains, their pollen is released in a sticky paste. This clings to the beetles' heads, ready to be carried to the next plant.

These flowers develop into sticky fruit covered in tiny barbs.

Silver thicket

(Euphorbia stenoclada)

This spiky plant with succulent stems belongs to the euphorbia family. This is a group of plants with milky sap often found in dry regions. The sap is poisonous to many animals and can irritate the skin, helping to ward off plant eaters.

The silver color comes from a powdery coating that may reduce water loss.

Bottle tree

(Pachypodium geayi)

Like baobabs, bottle trees store water in their trunks—but they also have sharp spines. The spines keep plant eaters away and catch dewdrops from fog. As the droplets grow heavier, they fall and moisten the ground around the tree, even during the dry season.

Octopus tree

(Didierea madagascariensis)

Named for its sprawling, tentacle-shaped stems, this tree has long spines to deter hungry herbivores. Among these spines grow narrow, conifer-like leaves that are good at retaining water.

These twisting stems can grow as long as 33 ft (10 m).

Animals of the Madagascan spiny forests

Much like its plants, Madagascar's animals are unlike any others on Earth. Around 90 percent of its animal species—including entire families, such as tenrecs, vangas, ground rollers, and lemurs—are uniquely Madagascan. This island was once joined to Africa and India but has been isolated for more than 80 million years—long enough to evolve very different wildlife.

Lafresnaye's vanga

(Xenopirostris xenopirostris)

Vangas are a group of Madagascan birds with different bill shapes. Some have long beaks for probing holes, others use needlelike bills for catching insects. This species has a stout beak, which it uses to chisel beneath bark for insects or to grab small lizards.

Spider tortoise

(Pyxis arachnoides)

This critically endangered reptile is restricted to the spiny vegetation along Madagascar's west coast. It spends the dry season buried in leaf litter, becoming active only when the rains arrive and plant food is easier to find.

The tortoise gets its name from the weblike pattern on its shell.

Lesser hedgehog tenrec

(Echinops telfairi)

The lesser hedgehog tenrec is one of more than 30 types of tenrec found in Madagascar. This dry forest species hibernates during the long drought. But even in the wet season, it stays hidden most of the time—waking for only about six hours after dark to climb through branches in search of fruit and insects.

Belalanda chameleon

(Furcifer belalandaensis)

Madagascar boasts more species of chameleons than anywhere else, including the world's biggest and smallest. The critically endangered Belalanda chameleon survives in just a tiny patch of the southwest. Its riverside forest habitat has been cleared, pushing it into nonnative trees far from its natural home.

Its grasping toes curl around a branch when climbing.

Madagascan dung beetle

(Scarabaeus viettei)

Dung beetles are common in tropical forests around the world. They roll balls of mammal dung, then bury them as food for their larvae. In Madagascar, where lemurs are widespread, this species mostly collects lemur droppings.

The beetle moves backward while pushing the ball of dung with its legs.

Its long, feathery tail is often held upright.

Long-tailed ground roller

(Uratelornis chimaera)

Madagascan ground rollers are weak fliers that mainly nest in burrows. They spend much of their time on the ground, searching leaf litter for insects. The long-tailed ground roller dashes across the sandy forest floor like a roadrunner, though the two are unrelated.

Lemur diversity

There are five families of lemurs, all of which are found in the forests of Madagascar. One family, made up of a single species called the aye-aye, lives only in the eastern rainforest. The other four families—sifakas, dwarf lemurs, sportive lemurs, and typical lemurs—include many species that inhabit different kinds of forests all over the island.

Coquerel's sifaka

Sifakas and relatives

The sifaka family includes 19 species, most of which live in Madagascar's eastern rainforests. However, some sifakas and woolly lemurs are specially adapted to the island's dry forests. All sifakas have powerful hind limbs for leaping through branches. The family also includes the tailless indri, which is the largest lemur in the world.

Sportive lemurs

These nocturnal lemurs leap through the trees like sifakas. All 25 species in this family are named for their quick moves—and perhaps for their tendency to pose like a boxer when threatened. They have an enlarged gut to help digest tough leaves.

Dwarf and mouse lemurs

The smallest lemurs are the nocturnal dwarf and mouse lemurs. This family of 36 species includes the world's tiniest primates. Many are found only in Madagascar's dry western forests, where some hibernate during the drought season—the only primates known to do so.

Aye-aye

The strangest lemur of them all, the aye-aye is a skilled insect hunter. Using its very thin middle fingers that are longer than the rest, the aye-aye probes and hooks the grub out with its claw-tipped hand.

Typical lemurs

This family of 21 species includes social lemurs that are active both during the day and at night. Most live in the eastern rainforest, but some western species, like the well-known ring-tailed lemur, spend more time on the ground than any other lemur.

Striped tail held high is a "follow-me" signal that helps group members stay together while finding food.

It uses one finger to tap branches and large ears to listen for grubs moving in hollow cavities.

Leaping sifaka

Athletic jumping helps tree-dwelling sifakas cover distances up to 39 ft (12 m) from branch to branch. But Madagascar's drier western forests are more open than the rainforests in the east. So sifakas here move between trees by leaping along the ground. In the spiny forests, Verreaux's sifaka does this by skipping sideways with its arms held high for balance—almost as if dancing in midair.

FACT FILE

Area
46,409 miles^2
(120,200 km^2)

Average rainfall
122 in (3,100 mm) annually

Average temperature
72°F (22°C)

Borneo montane rainforests

Home to our distant tree-dwelling relatives, the orangutans, Borneo sits across the equator in the heart of the tropics.

The world's second-largest rainforest island has some of the richest forests in all of Asia. From swampy lowlands to lofty mountains, these forests are as varied as the wildlife they shelter. Higher up on the slopes, montane forests, watered by clouds and rain, are hot spots of biodiversity.

Like many other ape species, the Bornean orangutan is critically endangered due to deforestation of its habitat.

Island apes

Orangutans were once found in tropical forests throughout Southeast Asia but now survive only on the islands of Sumatra and Borneo. They spend more time in trees than any other ape, so the rainforest habitat is critical for their survival.

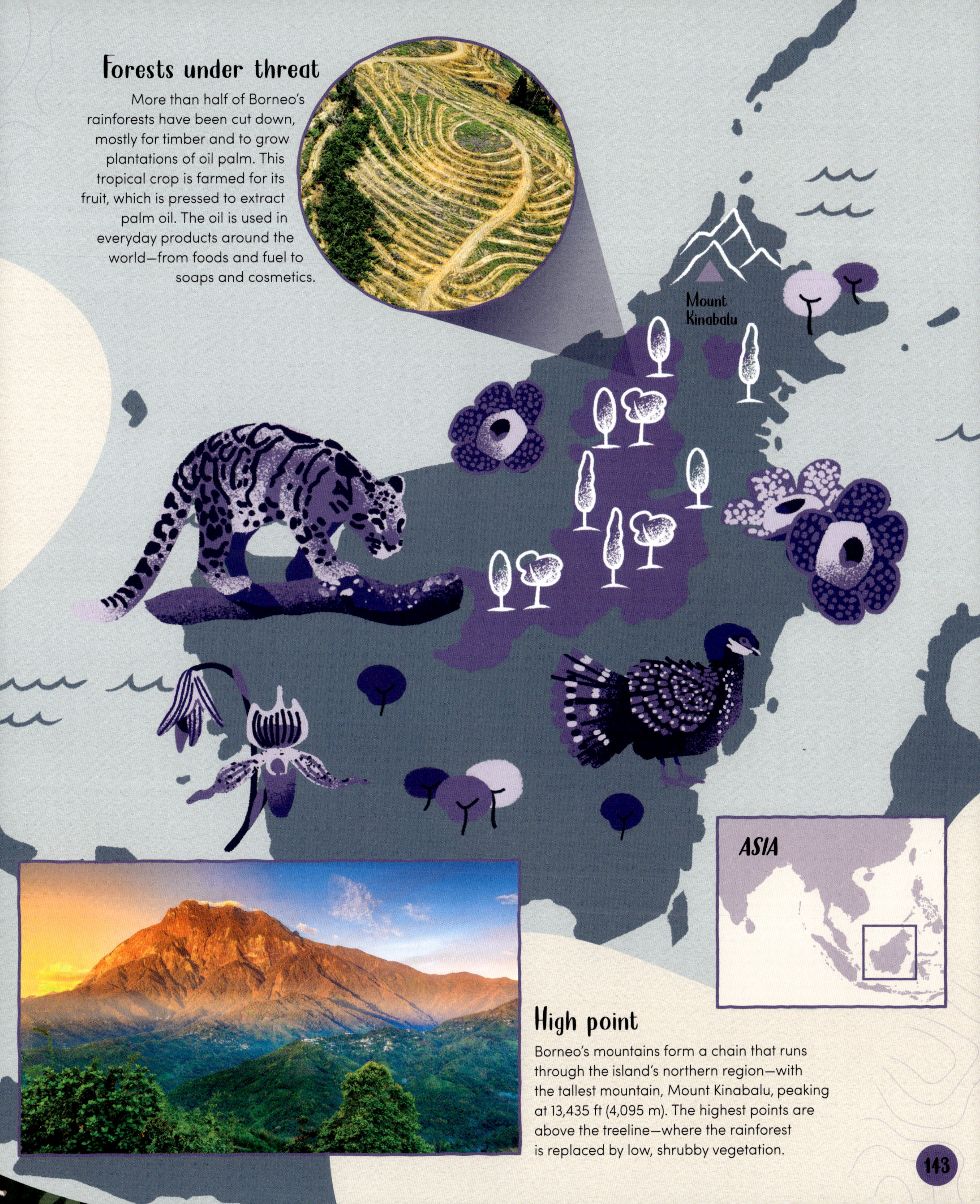

Forests under threat

More than half of Borneo's rainforests have been cut down, mostly for timber and to grow plantations of oil palm. This tropical crop is farmed for its fruit, which is pressed to extract palm oil. The oil is used in everyday products around the world—from foods and fuel to soaps and cosmetics.

High point

Borneo's mountains form a chain that runs through the island's northern region—with the tallest mountain, Mount Kinabalu, peaking at 13,435 ft (4,095 m). The highest points are above the treeline—where the rainforest is replaced by low, shrubby vegetation.

Geography of the Borneo montane rainforests

Borneo is the world's highest rainforest island, where landscapes range from white-sand plateaus to chalky pinnacles and hard volcanic rock. This varied geography has shaped the different forest habitats on the island. As the altitude increases, lowland forests give way to cooler montane rainforests.

Pinnacles between trees

Borneo's highest peaks, including Kinabalu, were formed from hard volcanic rock. But elsewhere, chalky limestone formations rise up among the trees. This landscape of jagged pinnacles, called karst, was formed over thousands of years as rainfall carved deep channels and caves into the limestone.

Mountain vegetation in the tropics

In many parts of the world, forest cover decreases from lowlands to highlands. This is because as the altitude increases, the air becomes thinner and colder, stunting plant growth. But the warmth of the tropics allows forests to grow higher on tropical mountains than on those in temperate regions.

Elfin forest

Trees are shorter on the mountains, where cooler temperatures and heavy cloud cover limit their growth. These twisted, fairytale-like trees give the "elfin forest" its name. A tangle of low branches thrives here, covered in moss that grows thick in the moist, foggy air.

Mountain forest soils

Soils are thin on the rocky peaks of Borneo's mountains, and nutrients are washed downhill when it rains. So many plants that grow here are specially adapted to cope with poor soil, including pitcher plants that trap insects for extra nourishment.

Plants of the Borneo montane rainforests

Midway between mainland Asia and Australia, Borneo's forests are home to plants from both regions. Some, like rhododendrons and dipterocarp trees, are more common in Asia. Others like podocarp trees have origins in the southern hemisphere. Cut off from the rest of the world, the montane forests became a haven for many species that exist only in this part of the world.

It produces large fruit with spiky skin and soft flesh.

Durian

(Durio dulcis)

The fruit durian trees has a strong smell—like a mixture of rotten onions, honey, and sewage. This might seem unpleasant, but many animals, especially orangutans, love it. The fruit of red durian has a creamy, caramel-like taste and is one of the sweetest durian varieties.

Montane corpse flower

(Rafflesia keithii)

Named for its stench of rotting meat that attracts pollinating flies, this leafless plant lives as a parasite inside a rainforest vine. Opening from a cabbage-sized bud, its flower is the largest in the world.

Its huge petals are dappled with the reddish color of raw meat.

The underside of the caps have unique honeycomb-shaped pores.

Luminous porecap

(Favolaschia manipularis)

This fungus grows in rotten wood, sprouting clusters of small white mushrooms. At night, they glow green, lighting up patches of the forest floor. Scientists think that this light may attract insects that help them spread their spores.

Mountain endemics

Most plant species in Borneo are endemic, which means they occur naturally in one place and are found nowhere else on Earth. These include mountain species of tree ferns, dipterocarp trees, and podocarps—tropical conifers with broad leaves instead of the thin needles that grow on conifers in colder regions.

Kinabalu podocarp

Montane dipterocarp

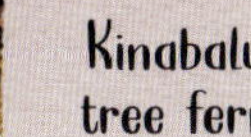

Kinabalu tree fern

Grass-leaved rhododendron

(Rhododendron stenophyllum)

Many plants on Borneo's mountains tolerate soils that are poor in nutrients and rich in toxic metals. Like other rhododendrons, the roots of this species partner with underground fungi to help it take in nutrients.

Drowned animals are digested in the pitcher, and their nutrients absorbed into the plant.

Giant pitcher plant

(Nepenthes rajah)

Borneo's montane rainforests host more kinds of carnivorous pitcher plants than in any other place, including the biggest of all—the *rajah* (king) pitcher plant. Its huge pitchers grow from tendrils at the tips of its leaves and can hold more than 101 oz (3 liters) of water—enough to drown rodents.

Growing about 12 in (30 cm) wide, it is often called " The King of Orchids."

Rothschild's slipper orchid

(Paphiopedilum rothschildianum)

Orchids make up one of the most diverse families of rainforest plants, and Borneo has at least 3,000 species. Unlike most other orchids, the rare Rothschild's slipper grows on the ground. Its pouchlike shape traps insects, so they brush against the pollen as they crawl out of the flower, helping it pollinate.

Forest regrowth

When lots of trees are cut down and large parts of the rainforest are cleared, the land gets scorched dry by the tropical sun. This makes it difficult for the forest to grow back. But in an untouched forest, trees topple over naturally. When they do, their fall triggers a process of regrowth that is vital for rainforest life.

Tree fall

No tree lives forever, and most trees in a tropical rainforest probably last only a few hundred years before weakening and falling over. Many have shallow roots, so wind, rain, and the weight of heavy climbers and epiphytes can make them topple.

Succession in a light gap

When a big tree falls in a tropical rainforest, it opens a gap in the canopy. Sunlight streams through this opening, reaching all the way to the forest floor. New plants grow upward to fill the gap, and different species slowly replace others in an ecological process called succession.

Primary and secondary forest

The canopy of a mature, or primary, rainforest blocks out so much light that little vegetation grows on the ground. However, in clearings and at the forest edges, the extra light encourages younger, thicker junglelike vegetation. This is called a secondary forest.

Primary forest
Older, taller forest has a more layered structure with less ground-level vegetation.

Secondary forest
Younger "jungle" forest is thick with branches and vines that are scrambling to reach the light.

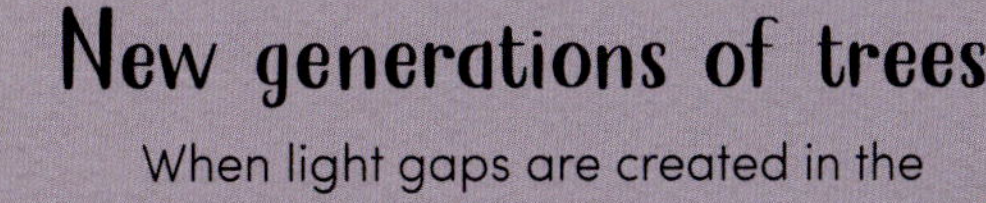

New generations of trees

When light gaps are created in the canopy, young saplings of the next generation of trees benefit the most. Some of them were already growing in the shade below. Others sprout from seeds that germinate once sunlight reaches the forest floor.

The flowers of dipterocarp trees grow better when they get direct sunlight.

Bornean orangutan
(Pongo pygmaeus)

Today, three species of orangutans live in the wild—one in Borneo and two in the neighboring island of Sumatra. All have reddish-brown coats, but Bornean orangutans have darker, shorter fur. The males also have wider cheek pads than those from Sumatra.

Orangutans have arms longer than their legs, helping them climb and swing through trees.

Chan's megastick
(Phobaeticus chani)

Stick insects are herbivores that live among vegetation, mimicking twigs and branches to hide from insect eaters. Restricted to Borneo, this species is one of the world's longest insects, with a body length of more than 14 in (35 cm).

Its long slender body is brown and green in color.

Animals of the Bornean montane rainforests

Borneo was once part of mainland Asia, before rising sea levels separated it as an island. However, many animals had crossed over by then. Today, Bornean monkeys, apes, treeshrews, leopards, magpies, flying frogs, and lizards still have their closest relatives in Malaya, China, and other Asian regions farther west.

Bornean peacock-pheasant
(Polyplectron schleiermacheri)

One of several ground-living peacock-pheasants found in tropical forests of Southeast Asia, this endangered species is restricted to Borneo. It lives on the slopes and ridges of the montane rainforest.

Wallace's flying frog
(Rhacophorus nigropalmatus)

Some species of Southeast Asian tree frogs are adapted for gliding between branches and are called flying frogs. Wallace's flying frog is one such kind. It catches the air using webs of skin between its long toes, which work like mini parachutes as it sails through the forest.

Their toes have large, round pads to cushion their landing.

Mountain treeshrew

(Tupaia montana)

Despite looking like large shrews, tropical Asian treeshrews are more closely related to primates. Borneo's mountain treeshew squats over pitcher plants to lap up sugary liquid from beneath the plant's lid. It poops into the pitcher, helping nourish the plant.

Both male and female birds are bright green and sport a black mask.

Bornean green magpie

(Cissa jefferyi)

This is one of many colorful bird species confined to Borneo's montane rainforests. The Bornean green magpie moves through the moss-covered undergrowth in search of food. It snaps up insects, snails, frogs, and even the occasional small snake.

Bartlett's flying lizard

(Draco cornutus)

Named after the Latin word for dragon, *Draco* lizards such as the Bartlett's flying lizard are small gliding reptiles that live in Southeast Asia. Of the 40 or so known species, many are found only in Borneo. Their ribs spread open to expand a gliding membrane that helps them "fly" between the trees.

Males use their colorful gliding membranes and throat flaps to defend their territory and impress females.

Dark-edged blotches on its coat look like clouds, giving the leopard its name.

Sunda clouded leopard

(Neofelis diardi)

Common leopards are found throughout Asian forests, but not in Borneo. Instead, the island's top predator is a smaller tree-dwelling relative—the Sunda clouded leopard. Compared to the size of its head, the clouded leopard's canine teeth are the longest of any cat—like those of the extinct sabre-tooth.

Buttress roots

In rainforests, most of the life-giving nutrients are found in the top layers of the soil, so tree roots do not grow deep into the ground. This shallow root system, combined with wet soil, can make towering trees unstable. To help them stay upright, the roots grow into wide, woody braces, called buttresses. They spread outward from the base of the trunk in all directions.

Glossary

ABUNDANT
living thing found in large numbers

ADAPT
when a living thing changes over time and many generations to become better suited to its surroundings

ALPINE
living high up on mountains, at a higher altitude than forests

BEDROCK
hard, solid layer of rock found deep beneath the soil

BIODIVERSITY
wide variety of living things found in a particular habitat

BLACKWATER
river or pool stained dark brown because of chemicals in rotting leaves, especially in the Amazon basin

BOG
open wetland with spongy acidic soil, created by flooding from heavy rainfall, often found in cooler climates

BROAD-LEAVED
tree that produces seeds from flowers, either evergreen or deciduous

BROMELIAD
any plant of the pineapple family, many of which grow attached to branches of rainforest trees

BROWSE
to feed on plants other than grasses

BUSHFIRE
wildfire that spreads quickly through bushes or woodland, especially in Australia

CAMOUFLAGE
the way a living thing is colored, patterned, or shaped to blend into its surroundings so it's hidden from its predators or prey

CANOPY
upper level of a forest, made up of the branches and leaves of neighboring trees forming a continuous layer

CONIFER
tree that produces seeds from cones, usually with evergreen, needlelike leaves

CONSERVATION
protecting habitats and the plants and animals that live in them

CRITICALLY ENDANGERED
species facing an extremely high risk of disappearing from the wild (*see endangered*)

CURRENT
a steady flow of water or air in a particular direction

DECIDUOUS
tree or plant that loses all its leaves for part of the year, usually during cold winter months or a dry season

ENDANGERED
species that is threatened with extinction and may disappear if it is not protected (*see extinct*)

ENDEMIC
a living thing found naturally in a particular part of the world and nowhere else

EPIPHYTE
plant that grows attached to another plant, especially those rooted to the branches or trunks of rainforest trees

EQUATORIAL
close to the equator, where the climate is tropical

EVERGREEN
plant that keeps its leaves all through the year and does not drop them completely during cold or dry seasons

EVOLVE
how living things change over time and many generations to generate new species

EXTINCT
species that has completely died out

FLOODPLAIN
low-lying land around a river that is flooded, especially during seasons of heavy rainfall

FOLIAGE
the leaves of a plant

FOREST
habitat made of trees growing so close together that their tops form a continuous canopy

GERMINATE
when a seed or spore starts to sprout and develops into a new plant

HABITAT
place where a plant or animal normally lives

HALOPHYTE
plant adapted to salty conditions

HEARTWOOD
the strong, dead, woody center of a tree trunk that supports the weight of the tree

HERBIVORE
animal that eats plants

HIBERNATE
how certain kinds of animals survive cold winters by entering a very deep sleep that slows down their body functions and lowers body temperature

INVERTEBRATE
animal without a backbone

KARST
landscape carved into limestone rock by rain, with many caves and channels

LEAF LITTER
layer of dead leaves on a forest floor

MANGROVE
tree adapted to grow on muddy seashores affected by the sea's tides

MARSH
wetland with lots of narrow-leaved grasses and reeds

MIGRATION
regular and usually seasonal journey undertaken by an animal for protection, feeding, or breeding

MONSOON
climate or region in the tropics with distinct rainy and dry seasons

MUDFLAT
land with a buildup of mud, especially around the mouths of rivers

MYCORRHIZA
partnership between a fungus and the roots of a tree or other plant, where they exchange nutrients

NATIVE
living thing found naturally in a part of the world and was not introduced there by humans

PEATLAND
wetland with thick layers of peat formed from the buildup of lots of dead plant material

PERMAFROST
underground layer of frozen soil that does not thaw out during the summer, and is found in the coldest polar regions

PHOTOSYNTHESIS
process where plants use light energy to make food from carbon dioxide, water, and minerals

PLUMAGE
feathers of a bird

POLLEN
usually tiny grains produced by male flowers or cones so a plant can produce seeds

POLLINATION
process by which pollen is transferred from flower to flower or cone to cone to fertilize a plant so it can make seeds

PRIMATE
group of mammals that includes lemurs, monkeys, apes, and humans

RAIN SHADOW
dry side of a mountain, created when clouds release all their rainfall on the opposite side

RAINFOREST
thick forest of tall trees found in tropical regions, where it rains a lot throughout the year

RESIN
sticky liquid made by some trees to help seal bark wounds and deter sap-sucking insects

RIFT VALLEY
long dip, or valley, in the Earth's surface, formed by the crust pulling apart

SAPWOOD
living outer woody layers of a tree trunk used for transporting water and nutrients up and down the tree

SHRUB
woody plant that branches close to the ground, rather than having a single trunk like that of a tree. A habitat made up mainly of shrubs is called shrubland

SOLITARY
living alone

SPECIES
specific kind of plant, animal, or other living thing

SPORE
tiny cell with a hard casing that can develop into a new plant or fungus

STAGNATE (AIR)
air that stops moving and stays in one place, often when it gets trapped by land or weather

SWAMP
wetland with lots of trees

TAIGA (BOREAL)
forest found around the cold northern polar regions, made up mainly of coniferous trees

TEMPERATE ZONE
region of Earth between the cold poles and hot tropics, with warm summers and cold winters

TIDE
rise and fall of sea level, usually occurring twice a day along coastlines

TISSUE
part of living bodies that performs specific jobs, such as photosynthetic tissue in leaves helps make food for the plant

TREE
woody plant with a single trunk that branches high above the ground

TROPICAL ZONE
region of Earth around the equator that stays hot throughout the year

TUNDRA
open habitat with short plants in the coldest polar regions, where the frozen ground stops trees from growing

VEGETATION
all the plants in a habitat

WETLAND
land that is flooded with water, either all year round or only for part of the year

WHITEWATER
river water clouded with sediment washed down from mountains, especially in the Amazon basin

WOODLAND
habitat made up of trees that are spaced apart so their tops do not form a continuous canopy

XEROPHYTE
plant adapted to dry conditions, with special features that help reduce water loss or store extra water

Index

Acknowledgments

DK would like to thank the following people for their assistance in the preparation of this book: Laura Gilbert for proofreading, Hilary Bird for indexing, and Samrajkumar S for picture research assistance.

The publisher would like to thank the following for their kind permission to reproduce their photographs:

(Key: a-above; b-below/bottom; c-center; f-far; l-left; r-right; t-top)

1–160 Dreamstime.com: Jackreznor (Topographic Background). **4–5 Alamy Stock Photo:** Danita Delimont / Christopher Talbot Frank. **6–7 MongaBay.com:** Rhett A. Butler. **8–9 Alamy Stock Photo:** Maximilian Buzun. **10–11 naturepl.com:** Jen Guyton. **12–13 Shutterstock.com:** Sunil Gupta. **14–15 naturepl.com:** Phil Savoie. **16 Alamy Stock Photo:** Afripics (cr); Universal Images Group North America LLC / De Agostini Picture Library (crb). **Dreamstime.com:** Mtilghma (cra). **17 Getty Images:** Corbis Documentary / Doug Wilson (cra). **18–19 Dreamstime.com:** Hbcs0084 (t). **18 Alamy Stock Photo:** Wildlife GmbH (l). **Shutterstock.com:** Gherzak (crb). **19 Adobe Stock:** Govinda (bl). **Dreamstime.com:** Photosimo (r). **22 Alamy Stock Photo:** Dinodia Photos / Indian Pictures RF (b); Derek Trask (cla); Derek Trask (cl). **22–23 naturepl.com:** Aflo (b). **23 Alamy Stock Photo:** Nature Picture Library / Constantinos Petrinos (cla). **25 Alamy Stock Photo:** Andrew Duke (bl). **Dreamstime.com:** Lyudmila Stozharova (r/x4). **Science Photo Library:** Dr Jeremy Burgess (tl). **26 Alamy Stock Photo:** Imagebroker.com / Florian Kopp (bl). **26–27 Alamy Stock Photo:** Blickwinkel / R. Bala (tc). **27 Alamy Stock Photo:** Imago / Chen Xiaodong (br). **Getty Images:** Moment / LeoFFreitas (cr). **Shutterstock.com:** Shahi Malik (clb). **28–29 Getty Images:** Moment / Simon J Byrne. **31 Alamy Stock Photo:** All Canada Photos / Stephen J. Krasemann (bl). **naturepl.com:** Doug Allan (tr). **32–33 Alamy Stock Photo:** CharlineXia Ontario Canada Collection. **33 Alamy Stock Photo:** Llukee (clb). **34 Alamy Stock Photo:** Bob Gibbons (t). **34–35 naturepl.com:** Konstantin Mikhailov (bc). **35 Alamy Stock Photo:** Don Johnston_NC (cl). **Dreamstime.com:** Sophia Granchinho (tr). **36 Doug Macaulay:** (tc). **Dreamstime.com:** Zuzana Randlova (b).

36–37 Alamy Stock Photo: All Canada Photos / Nick Saunders (tc). **37 Alamy Stock Photo:** Imagebroker.com / Gerhard Kraus (cra). **Shutterstock.com:** Matt Jeppson (cl). **Janet M. Storey:** (tl). **38 Alamy Stock Photo:** Minden Pictures / Donald M. Jones (tr). **38–39 Getty Images / iStock:** Cowtown Scribe. **39 AWL Images:** John Marriott (tr). **naturepl.com:** Mark Raycroft (br). **40–41 Getty Images / iStock:** Scalia Media. **42 Dreamstime.com:** Daria Pavlova (tr). **Shutterstock.com:** Evgenii Dagbaev (bl). **44 Depositphotos Inc:** Dimaberkut (br). **44–45 Depositphotos Inc:** Leonidikan (t). **45 Alamy Stock Photo:** Mauritius Images GmbH / ClickAlps (b). **46–47 Dreamstime.com:** Zastavkin (t). **46 Dreamstime.com:** Jolanta Dabrowska (bl). **47 Alamy Stock Photo:** Sergey Pristyazhnyuk (br). **naturepl.com:** Igor Shpilenok (tr). **48 Dreamstime.com:** Dmitry Potashkin (cra). **48–49 Dreamstime.com:** Zastavkin (b). **49 Alamy Stock Photo:** Wolfgang Kaehler (crb). **50 Adobe Stock:** Henri Koskinen (tl). **Dreamstime.com:** Miroslav Hlavko (cr). **naturepl.com:** Klein & Hubert (bl). **50–51 Adobe Stock:** Agami (tc). **51 Alamy Stock Photo:** Westend61 GmbH / Gerald Nowak (clb). **Dreamstime.com:** Aleksei Suvorov (cra). **52–53 naturepl.com:** Valeriy Maleev. **54–55 Depositphotos Inc:** ChinaImages. **57 Getty Images / iStock:** Lightphoto (crb). **Norbert Rosing:** (ca). **58–59 naturepl.com:** Jack Dykinga (b). **59 Adobe Stock:** Lost_in_the_Midwest (br). **60 Alamy Stock Photo:** Peter Martin Rhind (tr); Yonchee Photograph (b). **61 Alamy Stock Photo:** Danita Delimont Creative / Russ Bishop (r); George Ostertag (bl). **Getty Images:** Stone / Paul A. Souders (cl). **62–63 Getty Images / iStock:** Wildnerdpix (c). **63 Getty Images / iStock:** Gerald Corsi (cra); GaryKavanagh (br). **64 Dreamstime.com:** Nathan Hutcherson (tc). **64–65 Alamy Stock Photo:** Minden Pictures / Michael Durham (tc); NK Sanford (b). **65 Brian L. Sullivan:** (br). **Ron Wolf:** (cl). **66–67 Getty Images:** Moment / Colleen Gara. **69 Alamy Stock Photo:** David Broadbent (cr); @Diana_Jarvis (tl). **70–71 Alamy Stock Photo:** Craig Joiner Photography (t). **71 Getty Images / iStock:** Danielrao (br). **72 Alamy Stock Photo:** Nature Picture Library / Colin Varndell (t); Ian West (c). **73 Alamy Stock Photo:** Laurie Campbell (bl); Geogphotos (cla); Ernie Janes (tr); Andrew Kearton (br). **74 Alamy Stock Photo:** Blickwinkel / Cairns (tl). **SuperStock:** Imagebroker / Andrew Mason (bl). **74–75 naturepl.com:** Andy Rouse (bc). **75 Alamy Stock Photo:** FLPA (tl). **Depositphotos Inc:** Mikelane45 (cra). **naturepl.com:** David Kjaer (clb). **Shutterstock.com:** Peter Garrity (br). **76–77 naturepl.com:** Andy Rouse (tc). **77 Alamy Stock Photo:** Arterra Picture Library / Clement Philippe (ca); Nature Picture Library / Andrew Cooper (bc). **Getty Images / iStock:** Alphotographic (cr). **naturepl.com:** Klaus Echle (cra). **78–79 Getty Images / iStock:** Alex Manders. **81 Alamy Stock Photo:** Imago / Tao Ming (tc); Imago (bl). **82–83 Dreamstime.com:** Maciej Bledowski (c). **83 Dreamstime.com:** Light Fan (crb). **84 123RF.com:** Nakornthai (bl). **Alamy Stock Photo:** Tim Gainey (crb). **85 Alamy Stock Photo:** Botany vision (cb). **Dreamstime.com:** Ilona Lablaika (br). **Getty Images / iStock:** (t). **86–87 Getty Images / iStock:** Luxiangjian4711 (t). **86 Science Photo Library:** Steve Gschmeissner (crb). **87 Alamy Stock Photo:** Blickwinkel / Jagel (t). **Dreamstime.com:** Zepherwind (b). **88 Alamy Stock Photo:** Minden Pictures / Katherine Feng (bl). **naturepl.com:** Florian Möllers (tl). **89 Alamy Stock Photo:** Minden Pictures / Stephen Belcher (tr); Nature Picture Library / Wild Wonders of China / Staffan Widstrand (b). **Minden Pictures:** Ryu Uchiyama (cla). **90–91 Dreamstime.com:** Micha Klootwijk. **93 naturepl.com:** Juergen Freund (br). **94–95 Adobe Stock:** HansWismeijer (t). **94 Alamy Stock Photo:** Genevieve Vallee (bl). **95 Adobe Stock:** Christian Dietz (br). **96 Dreamstime.com:** Hilda Nerea Ogando Aricapa (tl). **Getty Images / iStock:** KarenHBlack (tc). **Shutterstock.com:** Metriognome (bl). **96–97 Alamy Stock Photo:** Nature Picture Library / Jiri Lochman (t). **97 Dreamstime.com:** Andreistanescu (cr). **Shutterstock.com:** Alybaba (bl). **Alfred Sin:** (cl). **98–99 Alamy Stock Photo:** Sindre Ellingsen. **98 Alamy Stock Photo:** Blickwinkel / F. Hecker (bc). **99 Science Photo Library:** Dr Jeremy Burgess (crb). **100 Alamy Stock Photo:** Auscape International Pty Ltd / Robert McLean (tl). **naturepl.com:** Suzi Eszterhas (bl); Martin Willis (c). **101 Alamy Stock Photo:** FLPA (cra); Minden Pictures / Roland Seitre (tc); Minden Pictures / Ch'ien Lee (br). **Depositphotos Inc:** MichalPesata (clb). **102–103 Alamy Stock Photo:** Auscape International Pty Ltd / Jean-Paul Ferrero. **104–105 Dreamstime.com:** Bidouze Stephane. **107 Alamy Stock Photo:** Gabbro (tr). **Dreamstime.com:** Mariusz Prusaczyk (crb). **108–109 Shutterstock.com:** Thiago Orsi Laranjeiras (t). **109 Shutterstock.com:** Best-Backgrounds (br). **110–111 naturepl.com:** Luiz Claudio Marigo (tc); Luiz Claudio Marigo (bc). **110 Shutterstock.com:** Nancy Ayumi Kunihiro (bl). **111 naturepl.com:** Theo Allofs (tr). **Shutterstock.com:** Guentermanaus (br). **112 Alamy Stock Photo:** Biosphoto / Quentin Martinez (cl); Nature Picture

Library / Sylvain Cordier (tl). **Depositphotos Inc:** Riverriver (bl). **112–113 Getty Images:** Gamma-Rapho / Sylvain Cordier (tc). **113 123RF.com:** Mariedaloia (c). **Adobe Stock:** Juerginho (tc). **naturepl.com:** Brandon Cole (br). **Shutterstock.com:** Bildagentur Zoonar GmbH (clb). **114–115 Getty Images / iStock:** Uwe-Bergwitz (t). **114 Alamy Stock Photo:** Juniors Bildarchiv GmbH / Schmidbauer, H. / juniors@wildlife (bl); Nature Picture Library / MYN / Martin Taylor (br). **Dreamstime.com:** Dennis Jacobsen (clb). **Bryan Kao:** (crb). **115 Aquarium Glaser:** (cl). **Dreamstime.com:** Rob Lumen Captum (tc); Mirkorosenau (cra); Mirkorosenau (cla). **naturepl.com:** Nature Production (tr). **116–117 Getty Images / iStock:** E+ / Gerald Corsi. **119 Alamy Stock Photo:** De Agostini / G. Sioen / Universal Images Group North America LLC (c). **Getty Images:** Jacob Silberberg (bl). **120–121 Shutterstock.com:** Muntaka Chasan (t). **121 AWL Images:** Will Gray (b). **122 Shutterstock.com:** Gilbert S. Grant (tl). **122–123 Alamy Stock Photo:** Mark Boulton (tc). **123 Alamy Stock Photo:** Juergen Freund (r). **Getty Images / iStock:** Agus Prianto (bl). **124 Alamy Stock Photo:** Danita Delimont / Alida Latham. **125 Alamy Stock Photo:** Juergen Freund (clb); VWPics / Jon G. Fuller (cla). **naturepl.com:** Shane Gross (tr). **Shutterstock.com:** Mikhael Johanes (cl). **126 Alamy Stock Photo:** Louise Murray (bl). **126–127 Getty Images / iStock:** Anakeseenadee (bc). **127 Minden Pictures:** Edward Myles (tr). **naturepl.com:** Doug Perrine (cr). **Shutterstock.com:** Francisco Herrera (cla). **128–129 Ger Bosma**. **131 Alamy Stock Photo:** Minden Pictures / Pete Oxford (crb). **Science Source:** Greg Dimijian (cl). **132 Alamy Stock Photo:** Hemis.fr / Montico Lionel (bl). **132–133 Alamy Stock Photo:** Imagebroker.com / Stefan Auth (t); Jim Keir (bc). **134 Alamy Stock Photo:** Nature Picture Library / Barrie Britton (bl). **Shutterstock.com:** Tarda Santo (tr). **135 Alamy Stock Photo:** Biosphoto / Jean-Philippe Delobelle (bl); Florapix (cla); Nature Picture Library / Lorraine Bennery (br). **Dreamstime.com:** Khairil Azhar Junos (tr). **136 Avalon:** Nick Garbutt (bl). **Shutterstock.com:** Lauren Suryanata (cb). **137 Alamy Stock Photo:** Agami Photo Agency / Dubi Shapiro (br); Imagebroker.com / Alexandra Laube (t); Luigi Carta (clb). **138–139 Dreamstime.com:** Luca Nichetti. **139 Alamy Stock Photo:** Imagebroker.com / Thorsten Negro (br); Nature Picture Library / Bernard Castelein (bl); Minden Pictures / Suzi Eszterhas (cb). **Ardea:** Geoff Trinder / ardea.com (tr). **naturepl.com:** Nick Garbutt (tl). **140–141 Science Photo Library:** Nature Picture Library / Andy Rouse. **143 Getty Images:** AFP / Romeo Gacad (tc). **Shutterstock.com:** Muhd Fuad Abd Rahim (bl). **144 Alamy Stock Photo:** Christian Loader (bl). **144–145 Dreamstime.com:** Sze Yun Lee. **145 Alamy Stock Photo:** Awgkuraem.photo (bc). **146 Getty Images:** Moment / Nora Carol Photography (bl). **naturepl.com:** Alex Hyde (crb). **Science Photo Library:** Dr P. Marazzi (tr). **147 Alamy Stock Photo:** Mick Klass (crb); Nature Picture Library / Adrian Davies (cl); Hulya Ozkok (br). **148 Alamy Stock Photo:** Anton Sorokin (cb). **148–149 Science Source:** Chris Gallagher. **149 Depositphotos Inc:** Imagebrokermicrostock (cra). **Getty Images / iStock:** PattayaPhotography (br). **Getty Images:** Andrea Pistolesi (ca). **150–151 Shutterstock.com:** Paolo Pako (tc). **150 Alamy Stock Photo:** Biosphoto / Quentin Martinez (bc); ImageBROKER.com GmbH & Co. KG / Arco / TUNS (tl). **Dreamstime.com:** Yezhenliang (bl). **151 Alamy Stock Photo:** ADS (tr); Nature Picture Library / Paul Williams (tl); Minden Pictures / Ch'ien Lee (c). **SuperStock:** Biosphoto / Alain Compost (br). **152–153 Alamy Stock Photo:** Nature Picture Library / Alex Hyde

Cover images: *Front and Back:* **Getty Images / iStock:** SStajic ca, Linas Toleikis t; *Front:* **Alamy Stock Photo:** ImageBROKER.com / Edwin Stranner b, ImageBROKER.com / Stefan Wackerhagen cb; **Dreamstime.com:** Sean Pavone bl; *Back:* **Alamy Stock Photo:** ImageBROKER.com / Edwin Stranner b, ImageBROKER.com / Stefan Wackerhagen cb